Quirky TRURO

CHRISTINE PARNELL
AND
SHEILA RICHARDSON

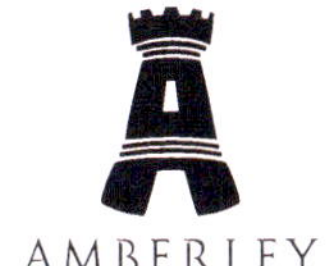

AMBERLEY

To my family with love – Christine

For Alan and Jenna with love – Sheila

First published 2025

Amberley Publishing
The Hill, Stroud
Gloucestershire, GL5 4EP

www.amberley-books.com

British Library Cataloguing in Publication Data.
A catalogue record for this book is available from the British Library.

ISBN 978 1 3981 2375 5 (paperback)
ISBN 978 1 3981 2376 2 (ebook)

Typesetting by SJmagic DESIGN SERVICES, India.
Printed in Great Britain.

Appointed GPSR EU Representative:
Easy Access System Europe Oü, 16879218
Address: Mustamäe tee 50, 10621, Tallinn, Estonia
Contact Details: gpsr.requests@easproject.com, +358 40 500 3575

Contents

Preface

Truro has evolved from a market town into a dignified cathedral city, but throughout its history many quirky characters and events have emerged. We are delighted to share our collection of stories with readers of *Quirky Truro*.

Our twice-weekly meetings at a coffee shop to write our script led the waiters to give us the nicknames 'Agatha and Enid', much to our amusement. It has been an interesting and happy experience as we met old and new friends who have been keen to regale us with various tales of our home town.

This book is about local events, strange happenings, tales of the unusual and, most importantly, the people both past and present who have had a positive influence on the town.

To us, Truro is home. There is nowhere we would rather be.

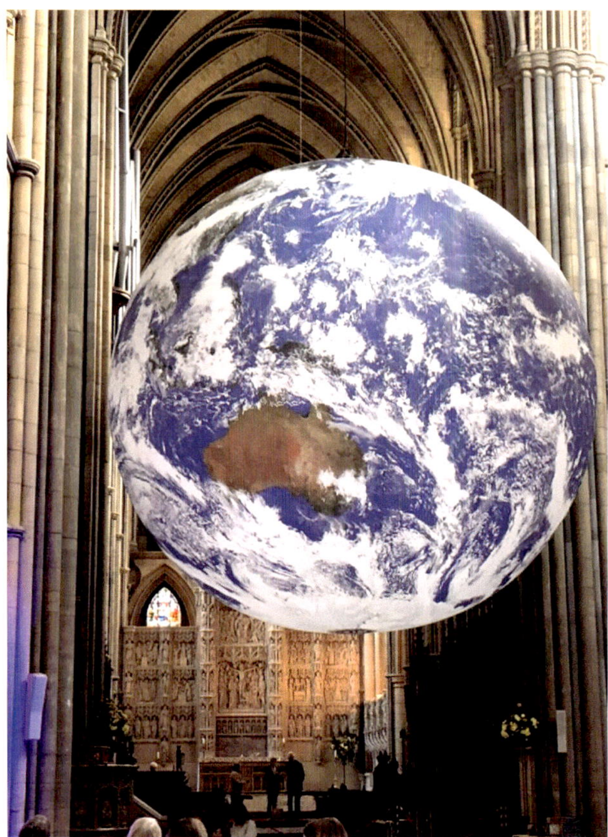

Gaia by Luke Jerram visited Truro Cathedral in October 2023. Measuring 7 metres in diameter, the installation allows us to see our planet floating in space as astronauts would see it.

Scenes of Truro

The Trafalgar Way

On 6 August 2005, to commemorate the Battle of Trafalgar and to honour the Cornish men who fought for their country, Truro City Council unveiled a plaque on a prominent wall in Lower Lemon Street.

The news of the victory of the Battle of Trafalgar was brought to Truro by Lieutenant John Richards Lapenotiere, the captain of the schooner HM *Pickle*. He landed in Falmouth on Monday 4 November 1805 to deliver the news of the victory, which was tempered by the announcement that Vice-admiral Horatio

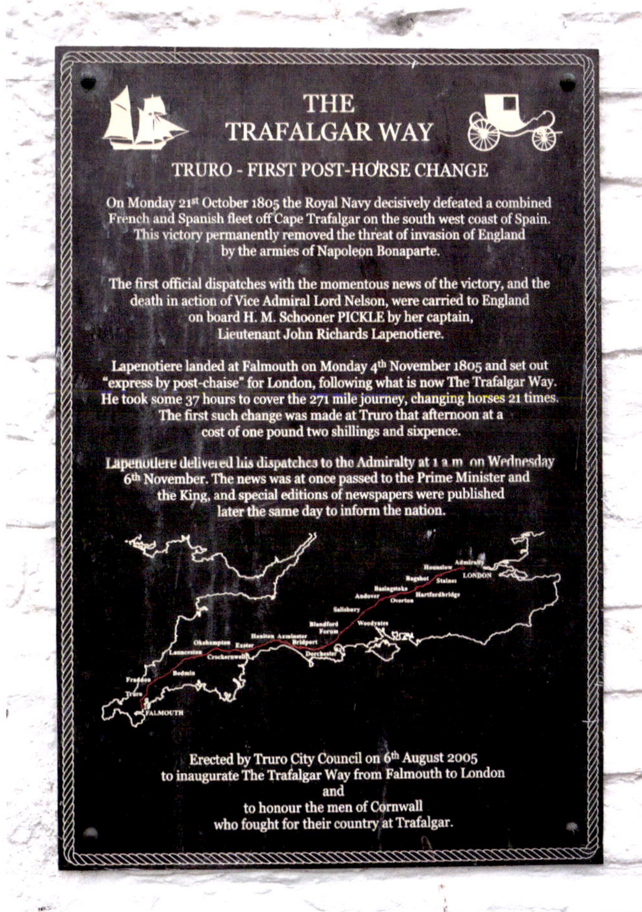

Situated on the wall in Lower Lemon Street, this is the first of thirty-one plaques marking Lapenotiere's post-horse changes on his journey to inform London of the victory at Trafalgar.

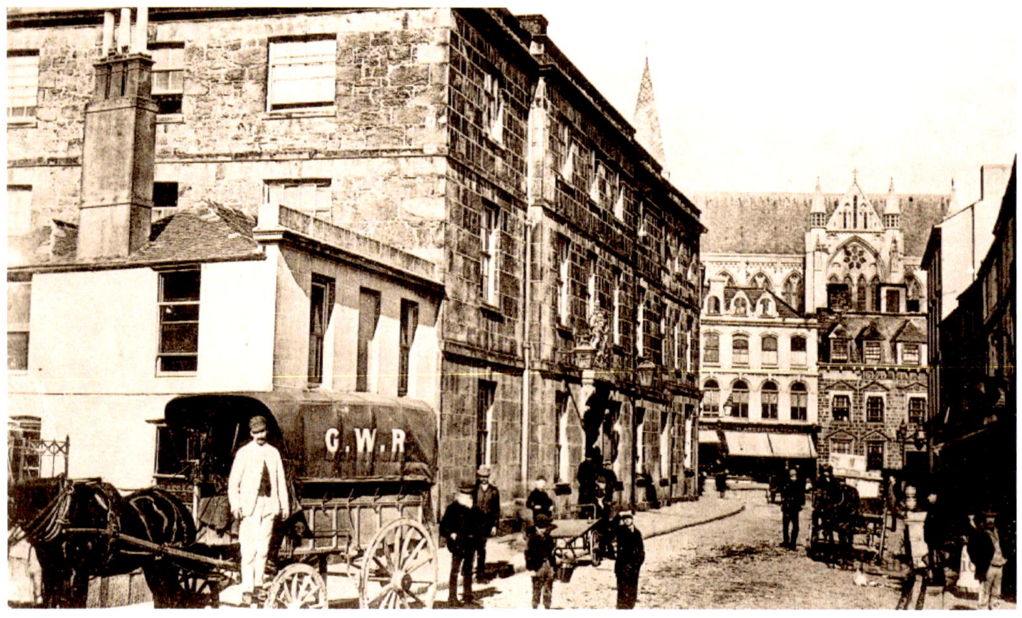

Pearce's Hotel (now the Royal Hotel) was the first stop on the Trafalgar Way.

Nelson had died in the battle. Lapenotiere's first stop was Truro, and he would change horses thirty-one times on his journey before reaching the Admiralty in London, where the news was delivered to Prime Minister William Pitt the Younger and King George III. Nelson's body, meanwhile, was brought home on HMS *Victory* in a cask of spirits of wine, having initially been preserved in brandy. Thirty-one plaques mark the route of the captain's journey from Falmouth to London, which is now known as the Trafalgar Way.

It was hoped in Britain that the victory at Trafalgar would remove the threat of a French invasion, but a decade later the country was engaged in the Battle of Waterloo against Napoleon's Army of the North. It took three months after that battle for the good news of a British victory to reach Cornwall, arriving on 10 September 1815.

On that same day, while the bells were ringing in celebration of the victory, William Bennett Bond was born in Truro. His family emigrated to Newfoundland when he was young, and in 1879 he became Bishop of Montreal. Greater fame awaited William in 1901 when he became Archbishop of Montreal and Primate of All Canada. A great day in history for Britain and for Truro.

Silvanus Trevail

Silvanus Trevail was a well-known architect born in Luxulyan in 1851 at Carne Farm. He was the son of John Trevail and his wife Jane, whose maiden name was also Trevail. From age seven to fourteen he went to the local school before moving to the private academy of Ledrah House in St Austell. A family story says that he was taunted by his classmates, who called him 'Silly Vain Ass'. He excelled in all subjects, passing examinations in the Junior Oxford and Junior Cambridge Certificates in 1866. The following year he passed the Senior Oxford Certificate and in 1868 he passed the Cambridge Senior Certificate, gaining honours in mathematics, drawing and constitutional history. Silvanus was able to style himself Silvanus Trevail AA after successfully passing the Associates of Arts examination of Oxford University.

Trevail's true fame came from his architectural designs, which spread not only throughout Cornwall but also across the nation. Locally, some of his prominent architecture includes the Truro Post Office which was at High Cross, the Passmore Edwards Library and the very grand Headland Hotel at Newquay. What was once Oscar Blackford's printing and bookbinding building (known in previous centuries as the 'Great House') needed internal redesigning, which he oversaw, along with the raising of the roof in 1903 to create an upper storey. At the time it was the composing room, but in later years it would be the bookbinding room.

When planning ceremonies for the laying of the foundation stone of Truro's cathedral in 1880, Silvanus was keen to welcome Edward, Prince of Wales in grand style. Instead of the usual bunting for this royal occasion, he planned five triumphal arches. Made of wood and plaster, they were each two storeys high and

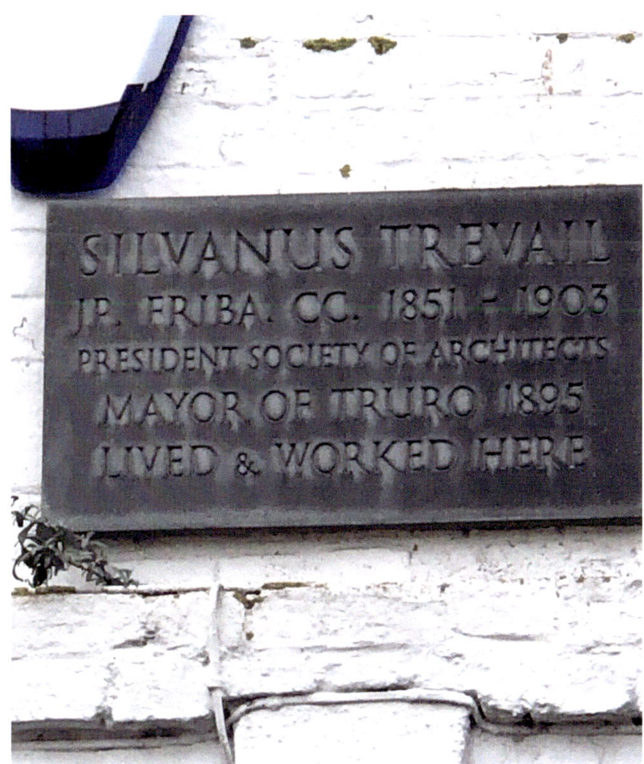

Silvanus Trevail, renowned architect of Truro, lived and worked at the site of this plaque in Lemon Street.

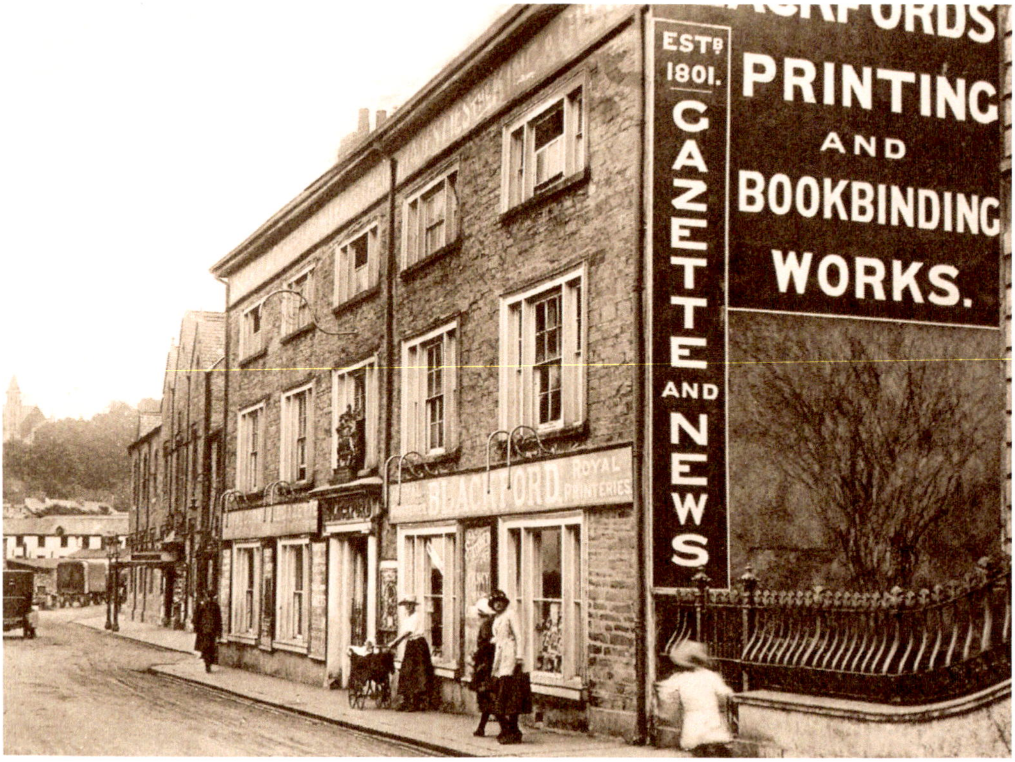

The Royal Printeries of Oscar Blackford, showing the royal crest over the entrance. This fine building was once known as the Great House and is believed to have been built by the Gregor family. (On the corner of King Street and Boscawen Street there was another town house by the same name which was owned by the Robartes family.)

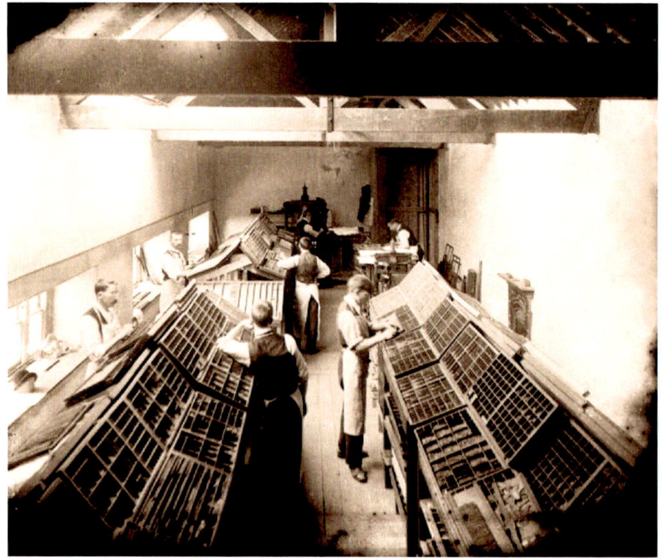

The Oscar Blackford building was redesigned by Silvanus Trevail. This is an early picture of the composing room, which was later moved to the ground floor alongside the printing presses. Although the compositors worked in a separate space from the print area, they still had to tolerate the noise from the busy printing machines.

boasted distinct architectural designs: Greco-Roman, Gothic, Tudor, Moorish and, of course, Cornish. They were strategically placed around the city at Boscawen Bridge, Lemon Street, Lemon Bridge, at the railway station and in River Street, which boasted the Cornish arch. This one had towers and battlements and bore thirteen medallions of the borough seals of Cornwall along with the arms of the distinguished Boscawen, Carew, Lemon and Trelawny families.

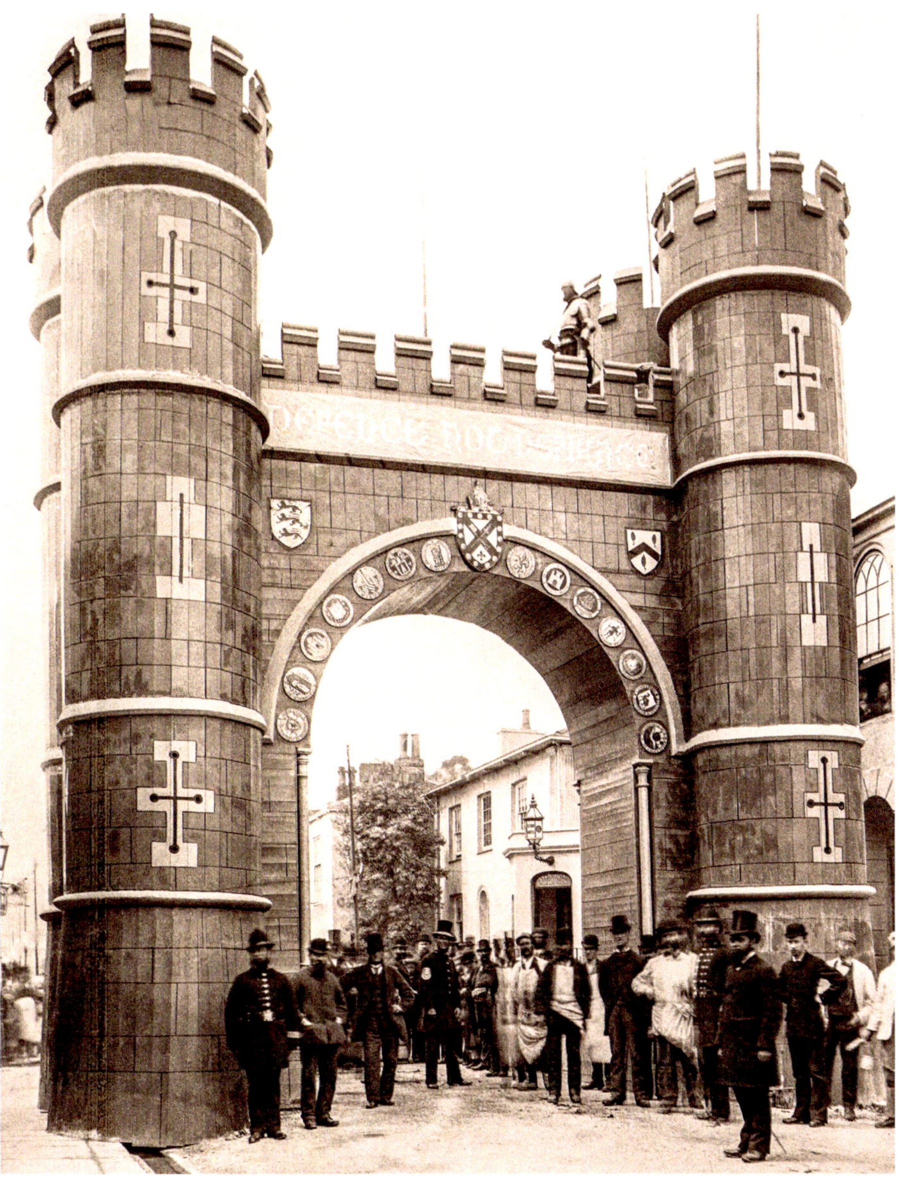

The Cornish Arch in River Street, one of five triumphal arches designed by Silvanus Trevail to welcome Edward, Prince of Wales to Truro.

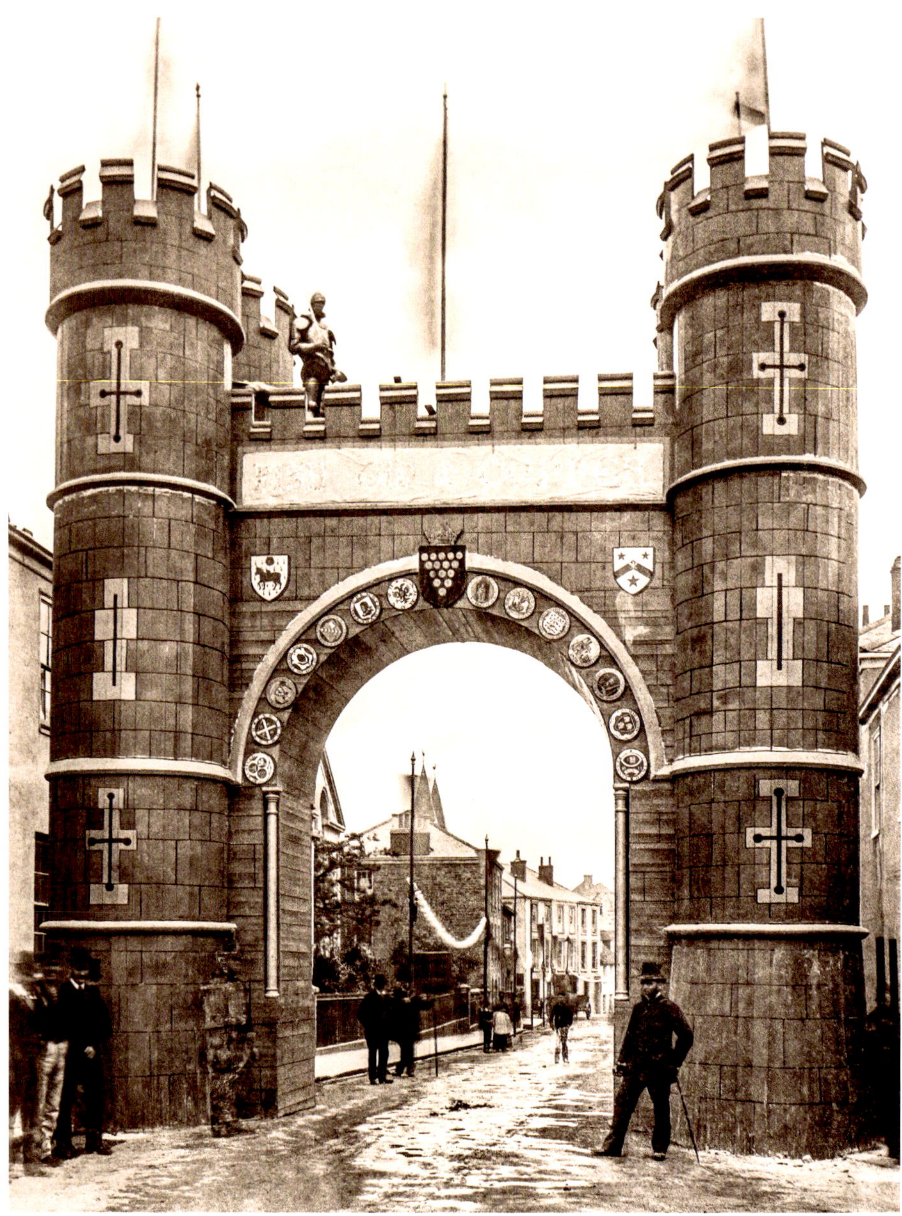

The opposite side of the Cornish Arch looking towards the town. Beyond the first chimney pots in the background, spires of the Congregational Chapel are just visible.

Trevail, besides many other distinguished titles, had also served as Mayor of Truro. Despite his outstanding career it is believed he had a history of depression, having lost his mother, father and uncle in quick succession. On 7 November 1903, wearing his familiar top hat and frock coat, he boarded a train at Truro bound for his uncle's funeral. He failed to get off at the correct stop, instead

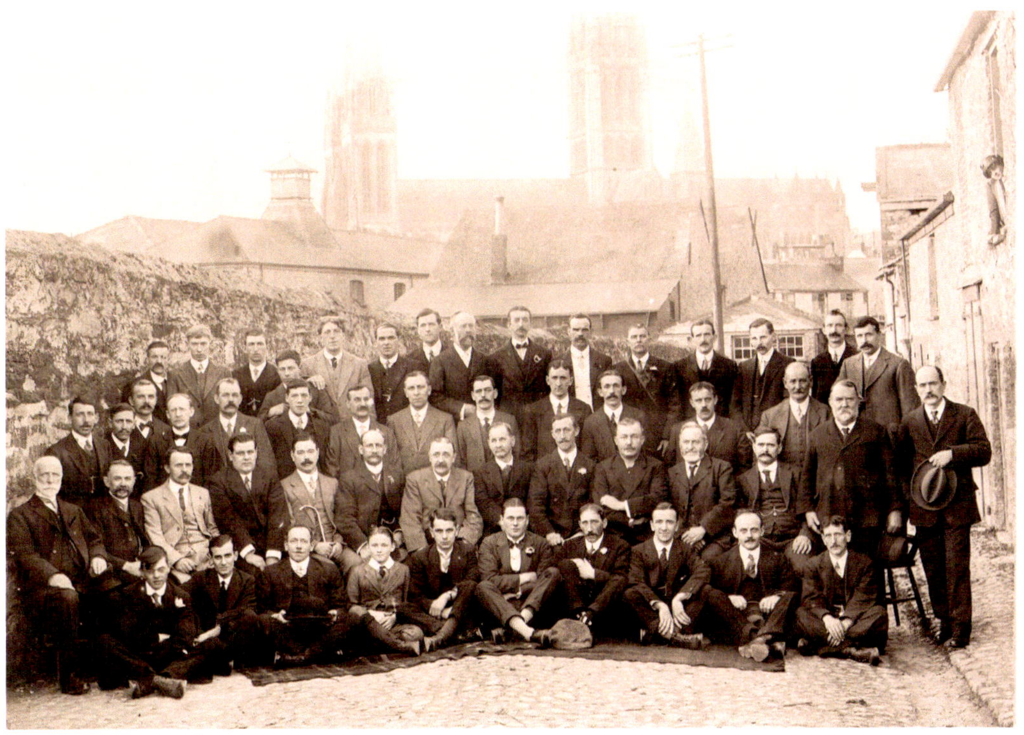

A group photo of Silvanus Trevail (second row from the front and second in from the right) and colleagues taken in Lemon Mews. We note the lady looking out of the window who did not want to be left out of the picture.

continuing his journey as far as the tunnel before Bodmin Road. As the train entered the tunnel, he went into the lavatory and shot himself.

Silvanus Trevail is remembered on a memorial plaque on the outside wall of his office at the bottom of Lemon Street.

Marching to a Different Beat

The Truro Piazza is home to one of the town's quirkiest but most controversial statues. Sculpted by Tim Shaw, this 15-foot bronze-and-tin statue is known as *The Drummer Boy*. At the time of the unveiling many Truronians were surprised to find this £95,000 addition to the piazza was in fact nude. The sculptor's explanation was that this reflected Cornwall's identity as a place 'marching to a different beat'. Also, the nudity meant the boy was not dated to any era. Drummer Roger Taylor of Queen fame was the special guest chosen to unveil the statue on 27 June 2011 because Truro was his childhood home. His early education was at Bosvigo School, where his first taste of music came with the group The Bubbling-over Boys. Roger attended Truro School and with his musical talent later became a member of Reaction. It was with his group Smile that eventually evolved into the world-renowned rock group Queen.

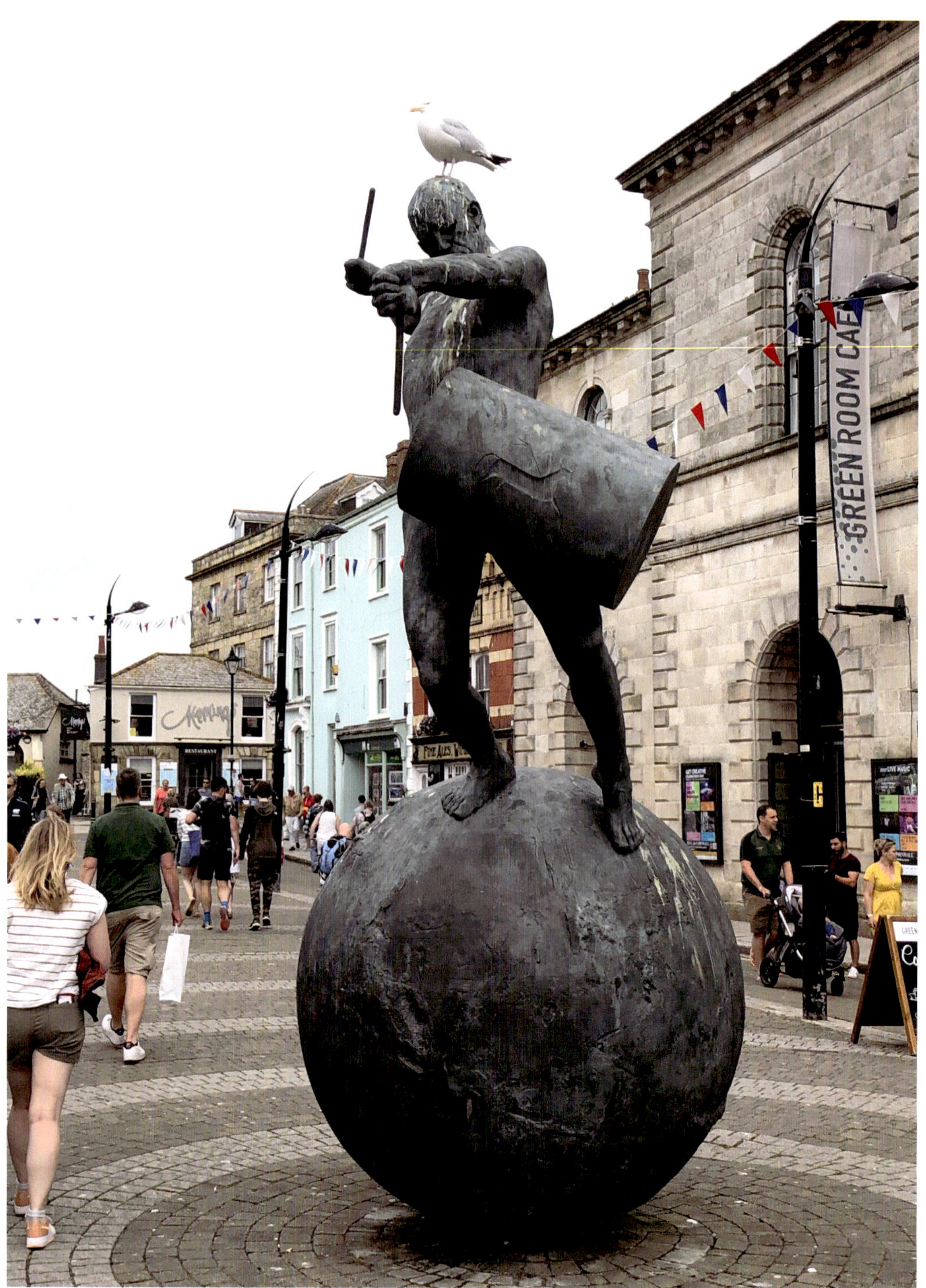

The Drummer Boy on the piazza is overlooked by a seagull. The statue was sculpted by
Tim Shaw and unveiled by Roger Taylor on 27 June 2011.

The unveiling marked another auspicious occasion as it took place forty-one years to the day after Queen, fronted by Freddie Mercury, made their first public performance at City Hall.

Celebrity Cats

Mr Jingles, the cat who delighted many occupants on Lemon Street and at various other places in town and also featured in our *Secret Truro* book, sadly died in March 2021.

Truro's friendly feline freely roamed his territory, visiting the Plaza Cinema and many offices and shops, where he received food and affection. He was sorely missed by his friends on Lemon Street, so a memorial plaque was made and now sits on the railings at one of his regular abodes.

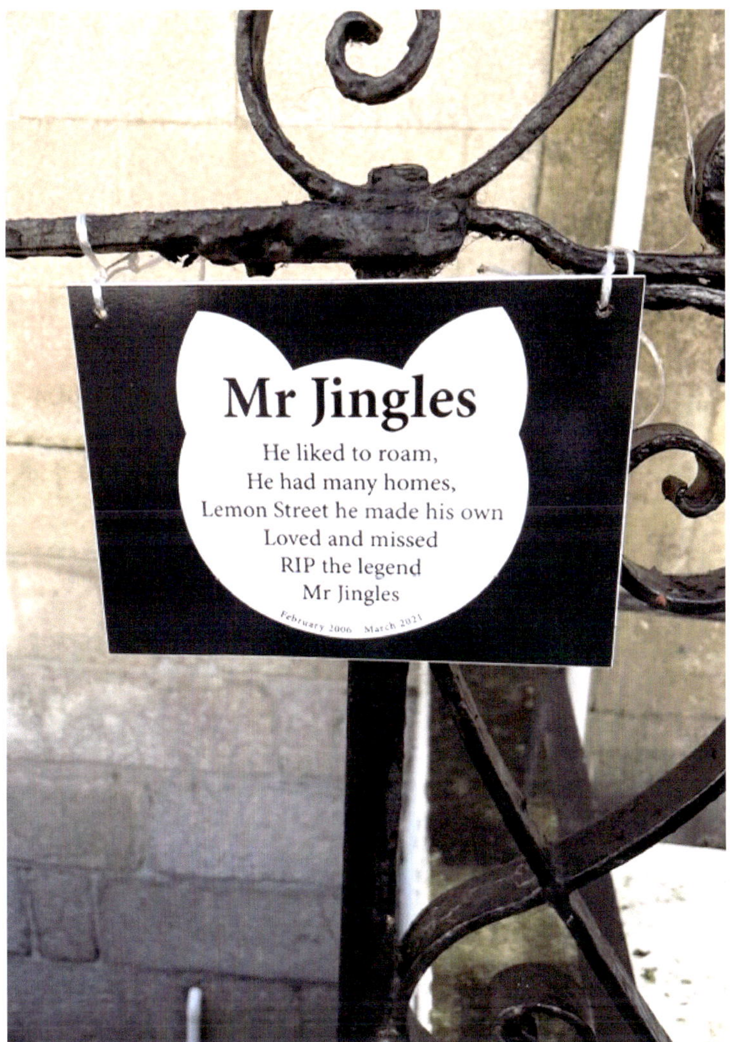

This memorial plaque of Mr Jingles on the railings in Lemon Street was erected by local residents who fondly remember the friendly feline.

Another feline who gained celebrity status in the town was Rusty, a ginger cat who could be found at Marks & Spencer as well as many other shops in the Lemon Quay area. When Rusty needed to get across town he happily jumped into people's cars for a free ride. He had also been known to sneak into premises unnoticed and on one occasion was locked in a shoe shop overnight. Mr Jingles and Rusty had been the talk of the town and were reported upon by locals on Facebook.

Muggins, meanwhile, was a big and beautiful ginger cat who lived in Bosvigo Road opposite the school. He was often to be seen sitting on the pavement and was a great favourite with the locals and the schoolchildren. One of his regular habits on a nice sunny day was to lie in the gutter and doze off. This caused confusion among visitors walking into town from the railway station who could be heard to say things like, 'Look at that poor dead cat' before Muggins slowly opened his eyes, yawned and went back to sleep. His other trick was to take one of his nine lives into his paws and snooze in the centre of the carriageway, but he was a lucky boy and never came to any harm.

Bob was another lucky ginger cat who came on a special visit to Truro. James Bowen and Bob were regulars on the London busking scene. James had little money and had just moved into some sheltered housing, while Bob was a hungry stray cat who needed some love and attention. James first saw him

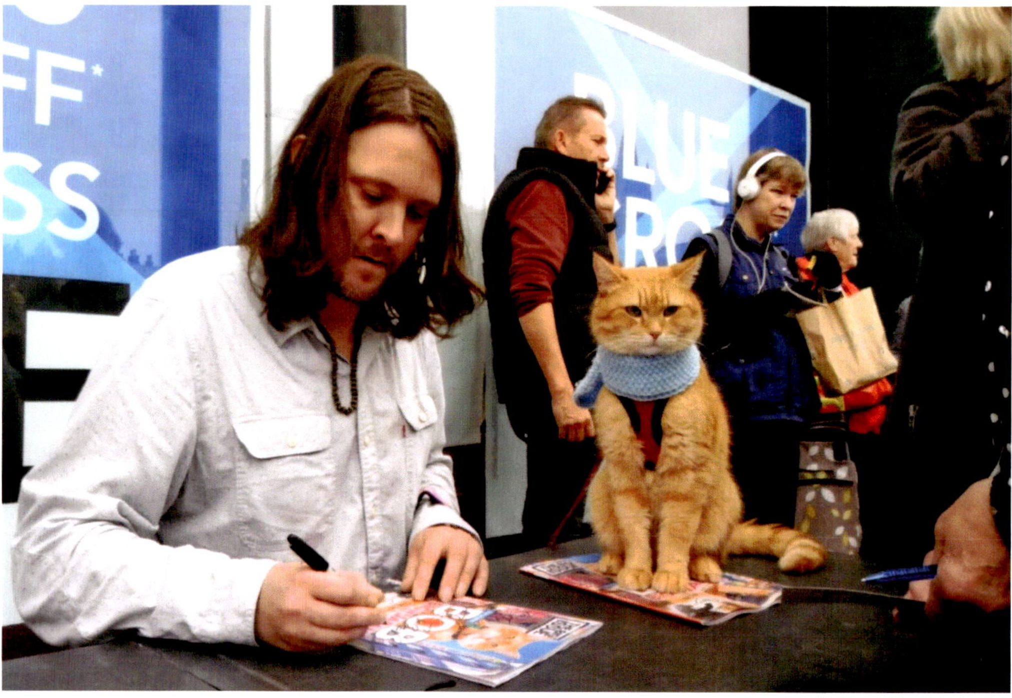

James and Bob, celebrity visitors to Truro, meeting admirers outside Marks & Spencer. While James is busy signing *Big Issue* magazines, Bob proudly looks on.

curled up on a doormat, and after several days realised that the ginger tom did not have an owner. He promptly set about getting some medical attention for the homeless cat, providing him with good food and love, and the pair became inseparable. Bob took to riding on James's shoulder while he walked to his favoured busking spot. Wearing a little harness, the cat would sit quietly on a mat beside the money box.

They became so popular that they regularly had crowds of people eager to see them. Before long, Bob had become famous all over the world. He received fan packages with far too many treats for him to manage, so James donated them to rescue centres for other needy felines. Now famous, James actively helped to promote *The Big Issue* so that others in the position he had been in could sell the magazine and hopefully have 'a hand up, not a handout'.

Bob's fame led him to visiting other countries, and in 2017 the duo toured Japan. What could come next after the excitement of Japan? Well, how about Truro!

Truronians were used to seeing a man named Nick selling his copies of *The Big Issue* on the piazza outside Marks & Spencer, but excitement grew when James and Bob arrived to join him. A large and happy crowd arrived, the television cameras were set up and James signed copies of the magazine for customers while the beautiful Bob sat on a table watching every movement of his admirers and loving the attention. He was truly a celebrity cat.

Christmas Pyramid Grill

Christmas on Truro's Piazza has for the last nine years been a colourful and delightful event thanks to the arrival of the Pyramid Grill at the start of the festive season. This tall, four-tiered structure with rotating windmill-style arms is an imposing feature. Within the upper tiers are life-sized models of the Nativity, with the Three Kings on the tier below, while food is cooked at the base. The whole pyramid is illuminated and complements the town's Christmas decorations.

The Pyramid Grill is the brainchild of Maxine and her husband Shane, who run the Plymouth business Rowlands Catering Co. Ltd.

After visiting the famous German Christmas markets, Shane decided to build a pyramid in an authentic German style and drew the sketches for it himself. With the help of his cousin Thomas, they built this Christmas pyramid in three months. On completion it was checked by a structural engineer and exhibited for the first time in Plymouth – to the delight of the Plymouth town manager, who also happened to be from Germany. Plymouth Council were not interested in hosting it the following year, and when Truro heard Shane was looking for a new venue they were thrilled and welcomed the pyramid to the piazza.

Maxine and Shane are event catering specialists who provide their services throughout the year, visiting various traditional festivals in towns throughout Devon and Cornwall, but the Pyramid Grill comes only to Truro, where it is welcomed by customers and friends.

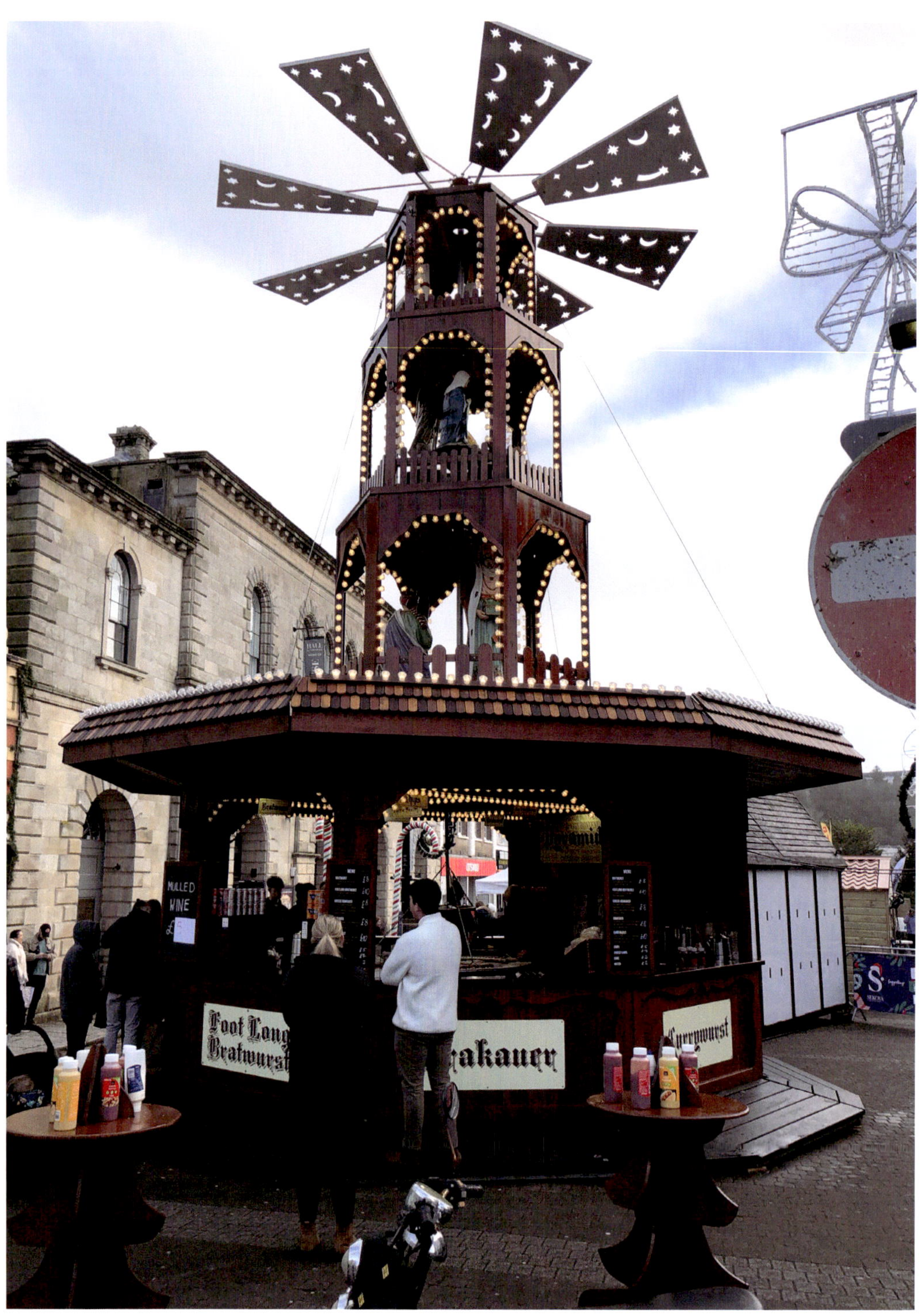

The Christmas Pyramid Grill on its annual visit to Truro in December 2023.

Fiery Steve

The story of Fiery Steve has come to our pages thanks to the research of two local men who set out in 2014 to test the width of Squeeze Guts Alley by trying to pass each other down that walkway. The alley is said to be one of the narrowest passages in the country and is known to have caused many persons of large girth to get stuck, including Sir Cyril Smith MP.

Whispers have it that this 'ope', which stretches from St Mary's Street to Duke Street, also has a haunted tale to tell, and so the two men did some digging and found the following story.

Squeeze Guts Alley is believed to be haunted by Steven H. Treffry, who fell to his death on 20 December 1787. Twenty-seven-year-old Steven was a carpenter and gilder by trade and had his workshop at the Duke Street end of the passage, with sleeping quarters above. His parents used to have a vegetable business in Middle Row, and Steven was a well-known and liked person of the town.

When there was work available at the dockside, a bell was sounded and there would be a mad rush of locals eager to earn some money. Duke Street Passage, as Squeeze Guts Alley was named then, was a noisy alley because it was a shortcut to the docks through other opes in the town. It was also very noisy at night when inebriated locals rolled out of the public houses and entertainment venues. This in particular annoyed Steven so much that he would take red-hot coals from his fire and throw them down on the noisy characters below. So frequent an occurrence

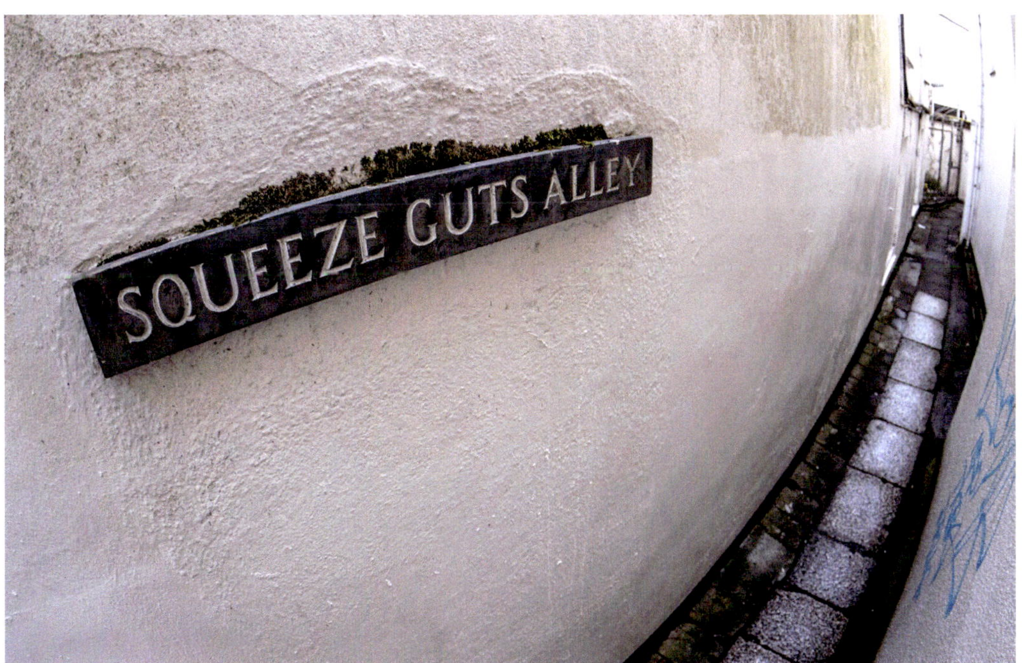

Squeeze Guts Alley, a famously narrow passage, is believed to be haunted by Steven Treffry (alias Fiery Steve), who fell to his death here.

was this that the parish constable, John Bolitho, regularly had to lock Mr Treffry in the town prison.

On this sad occasion, however, Steven had not realised that some of the hot coals from his shovel had fallen on to the floor in his room. While he was shouting at the noisy people below, a fire broke out in the room. He attempted to put out the flames, but instead his nightshirt caught alight. Terrified and enveloped in flames, he ran to the window that overlooked the passage and sadly fell to his death. Two brothers, George and Peter Richards, helped to put out the flames but too late to save Steven Treffry.

Although it is unknown who wrote the following verse, it is a reminder of the alley being haunted:

Fiery Steve
If, on a fine Midsummers Eve
Through Squeeze Guts Alley you should stray
Please be aware of Fiery Steve
Who haunts the ope upon that day

Whether you are someone of generous size or simply scared of ghosts, Squeeze Guts Alley is definitely a place to approach with caution.

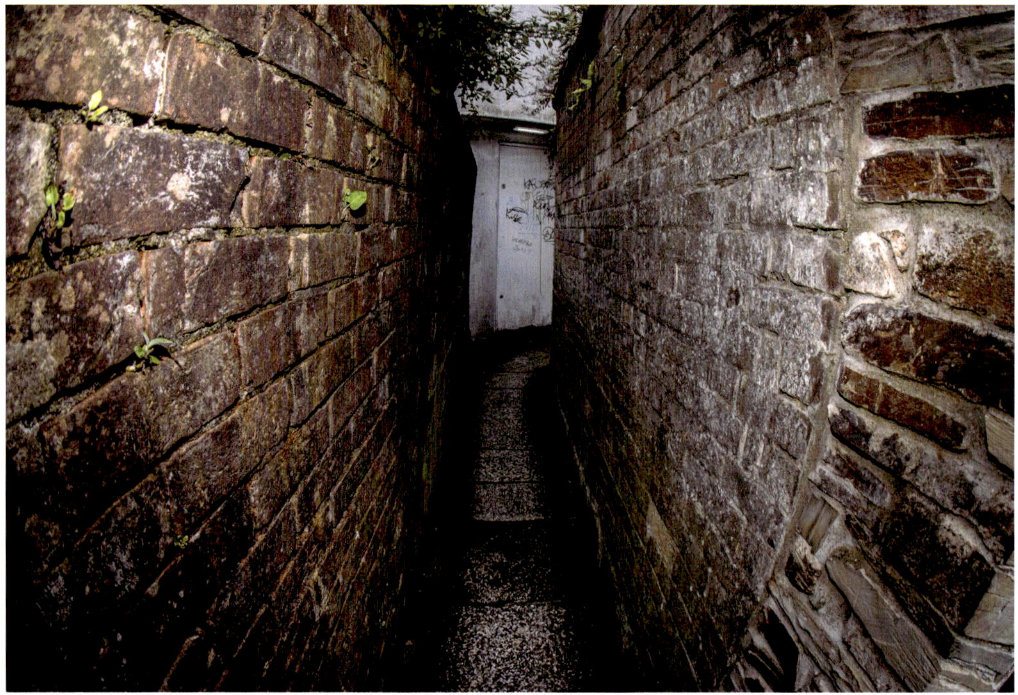

The narrow and dark end of Squeeze Guts Alley approached from St Mary's Street is still a well-used shortcut for busy shoppers today.

Famous Fellows and Firm Foundations

John Wolcot

John Wolcot was born in Devon in 1738, but after his father died he was educated in Bodmin. He then went to live in Fowey with his uncle, who was a surgeon. He became his uncle's apprentice and completed his medical training in 1767 in Aberdeen. He then went to Jamaica as physician to its governor, Sir William Trelawny, and while there he became an ordained member of the Church. A few years later, on the death of Sir William, he returned to England, gave up his faith and settled in Truro as a doctor. He was friend to many of Truro's elite and was welcomed in their houses; Thomas Daniell, the owner of a property that still exists today as the Britannia Inn, allowed Wolcot to live at his place rent free. At this time he also attempted to support the burgeoning careers of painters Henry

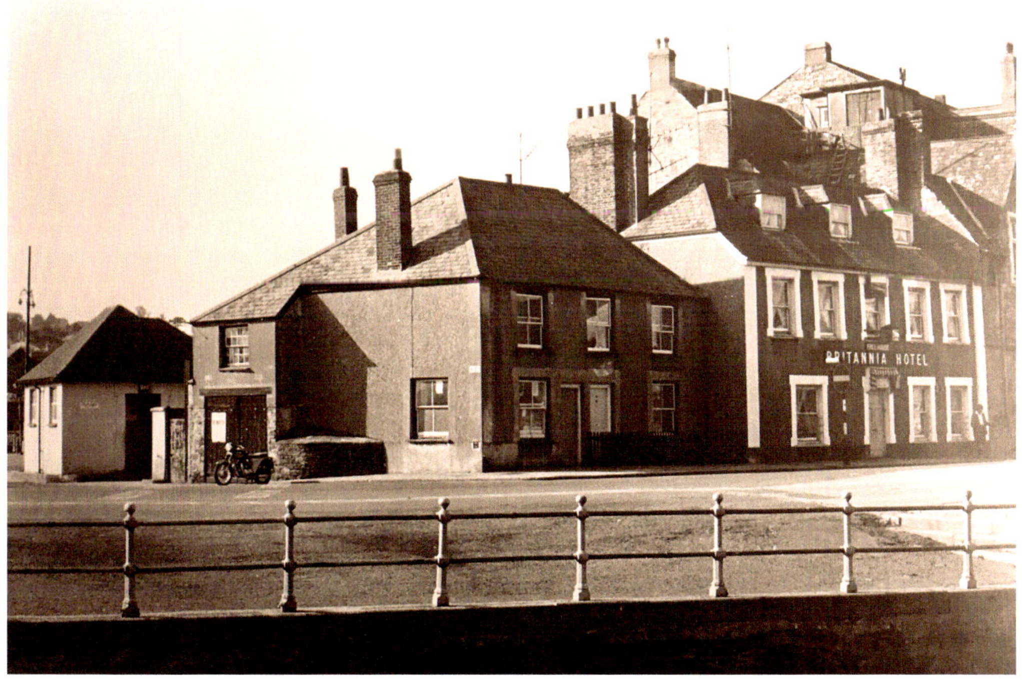

The Britannia Hotel was the home of John Wolcot, who was allowed to live there rent free by Thomas Daniell.

Bone and John Opie, although he might have had his own ambitions in mind when he brought them to London.

Wolcot's welcome among the local elite soon began to sour, however, when he began writing satirical verses in which he poked fun at them under the nom de plume of Peter Pindar. In Truro, the mayor and corporation were often targets; further afield, he did not spare the feelings of the court or royalty.

In 1778, John Buckland 'the perpetual overseer of the poor', informed Wolcot that he was obliged to take an apprentice from the parish. Wolcot took himself off to Helston and replied to the demand, stating that if they insisted on placing an apprentice at his house then Mr Buckland should go to his house in the company of the mayor and deputy recorder and instruct them to put the apprentice through the keyhole. The mayor and corporation felt that John Wolcot had been disrespectful, and the town clerk was instructed to write to Wolcot asking him apologise within four days. Instead, the mayor received one of Wolcot's satirical verses. The first few lines went as follows:

> The Sages met in full Divan
> To wreak dire vengeance on the man
> Who to John Buckland wrote epistle
> Bidding the Alderman go whistle.

John Wolcot died at Somers Town, London, in 1819.

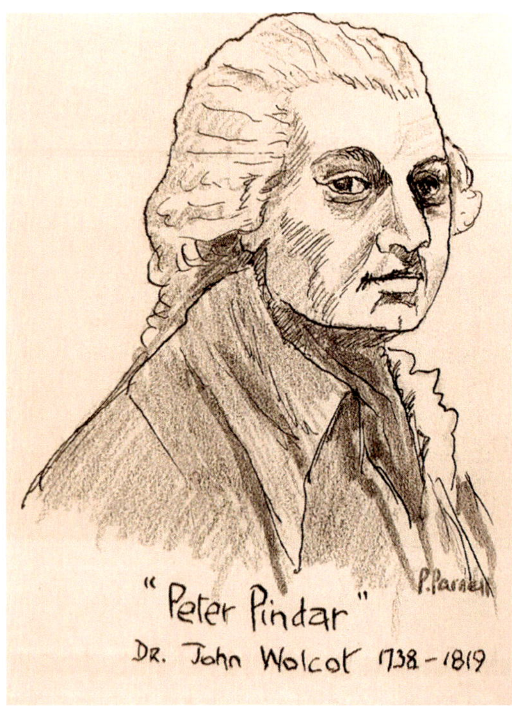

John Wolcot was mentor of John Opie and Henry Bone. Wolcot wrote satirical verses under the pseudonym Peter Pinder.

Henry Bone

Henry Bone was born in Truro in 1755. He came from a talented family as his father was not only a cabinetmaker but also excelled at wood carving – he was responsible for the pulpit in St Mary's Church, at that time known as Truro Church, which is a feature of St Mary's Aisle in the cathedral today.

When he was sixteen, Henry was apprenticed to William Cookworthy in Plymouth and he became familiar with hard-paste porcelain. The business moved to Bristol and Henry went too, honing his ability to draw and paint on porcelain all the while, but when Cookworthy's business failed after Henry had been

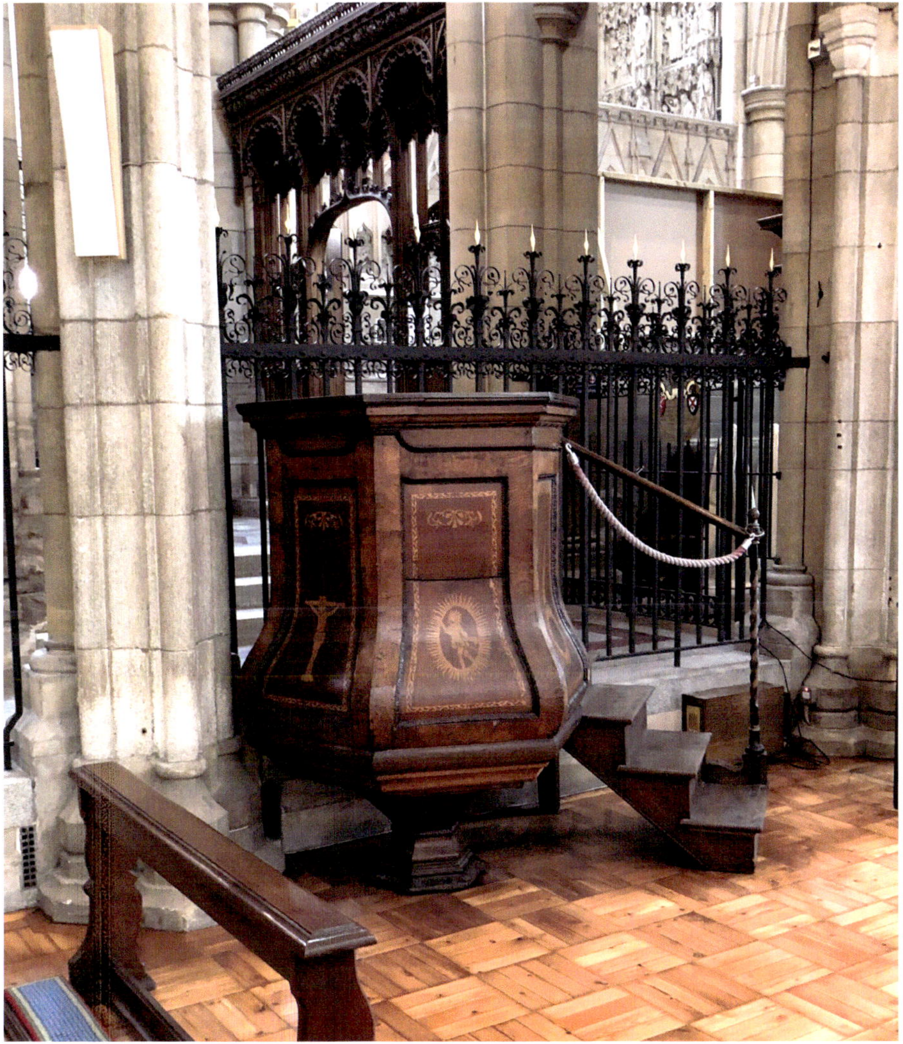

This wooden pulpit was carved by Henry Bone's father. Originally located in the central aisle of St Mary's Church, it was moved to the south aisle when the central aisle was demolished to become part of the new cathedral.

with him for six years he made his way to London. Henry was not well off, but fortunately he crossed paths with our friend Dr John Wolcot, who became his guide and helped him start a career in the capital.

Bone's work was stunning. To this day he is acknowledged as possibly the very best at his art. He was appointed enamellist to George III, George IV and William IV, and his exquisite work brought him fame and membership of the Royal Academy. He died in 1834, but he had lived long enough to see his namesake son, Henry Pierce Bone, honoured as enamel painter to Queen Victoria in 1833.

Although Henry produced hundreds of miniature enamels, he broke convention by making a few larger works. Much of his work is tucked away in private collections, but his portrait of George Washington made it across the Atlantic and today hangs proudly in the White House.

William Gregor

Christmas Day 1761 was extra special for Mary and Francis Gregor, who lived at Trewarthenick near the beautiful church at Cornelly in the parish of Creed. On this day, their younger son William was born. As he grew up, it became clear that William had a keen interest in chemistry. This was not to be his occupation, however, as after grammar school in Bristol he eventually went up to Cambridge to become a man of the cloth. He could have attained high office in the Church but decided that he would prefer to be the rector of a parish in Devon, near Totnes. In 1793 he accepted a living from the Bishop of Exeter – a relative of his wife – and soon he was able to change it for the living of Creed. He had worked his way home.

William still retained his love of chemistry, and in 1791 a friend, knowing how talented he was, sent him some black sand from Manaccan to see what he could find out about it. Having performed many experiments on it, William found that iron oxide made up half of the sample. He deduced that the other half was the oxide of another metal, but he did not know what metal it could be and so gave it the name manaccanite. His findings, printed in a German publication, went unnoticed. It was not until 1795 that Martin Heinrich Klaproth, a scientist from

This titanium plaque commemorates the identification
of the metal menachanite, later called titanium,
by the Reverend William Gregor
in the Leat of Tregonwell Mill,
in the Parish of Manaccan in Meneage in 1791.
It also acknowledges
the work of
Professor Per-Ingvar Brånemark, MD. PhD. of Göteborg, Sweden,
who in the 20th century pioneered the use of titanium
in reconstructive surgery
allowing the permanent attachment of artificial
teeth and limbs directly to bone by osseointegration

This plaque on a wall at Tregonwell Mill commemorates Reverend William Gregor.

Berlin, discovered the same oxide in samples of a red ore from Hungary and named it titanium. Klaproth was generous enough to share the recognition with William, who had discovered it first, but titanium was the name that stuck.

William Gregor had many qualities. An excellent parish priest, he also painted, drew and played the piano; although he was nationally acclaimed as a chemist, he regarded it only as a hobby. He died at the age of fifty-five in 1817.

John Opie

In 1761, John Opie was born in Mithian in the parish of St Agnes. His father was a builder and carpenter and he always intended his son to follow in his footsteps, but John's mother and his uncle soon recognised the boy's talent for drawing and also for mathematics. By twelve he had mastered Euclid and was teaching evening maths classes at the local school, helping many people, including adults. His drawings of local characters were well known and respected and brought him to the attention of Dr John Wolcot, who took the boy to live with him in his Truro home where he had the run of the house. He equipped Opie with artist's pens, pencils and canvasses, and eventually brought him to the capital and introduced him to London society (among them Sir Joshua Reynolds) as 'the Cornish Wonder'.

Opie was popular and successful. Becoming a member of the Royal Academy, he exhibited 143 paintings in all. He was a Professor of Paintings and he also gave lectures. Fortunately, he painted twenty self-portraits over the years, so we know what he looked like. He became ill in 1807 and, despite the care of his wife and sister, he sadly died at the age of forty-six. His funeral was a huge and an impressive affair attended by many dignitaries and aristocrats, including Lord De Dunstanville and Sir John St Aubyn. Mourners who were unable to attend sent carriages emblazoned with their coats of arms as a mark of respect. He was buried in the crypt of St Paul's Cathedral near to his friend Sir Joshua Reynolds.

In the early years of the twenty-first century, two members of the Truro Old Cornwall Society finished a tour of St Paul's Cathedral and sank gratefully onto chairs in the cathedral's café. While having her lunch, one of them looked down and saw the words 'St Agnes' between her feet. Her husband immediately moved the chairs to reveal the tombstone of John Opie. The lady thought she should bring John up to date, and so told him about how his home was doing.

Much later, after attending a talk about John Opie by the expert Viv Hendra, the same lady told him about the tombstone under her feet. Mr Hendra laughed and surprised everyone with his explanation: 'Through some accident John Opie was buried the wrong way round, so you were talking to his feet!'

Henry Martyn

The Baptistry of Truro Cathedral is dedicated to Henry Martyn, who was born in Truro in 1781. Unfortunately his name is not as well known as it deserves to be for his missionary work and Bible translations. Sadly, his mother died giving birth to his sister Sally. His father, who was a caring man, realised that his son

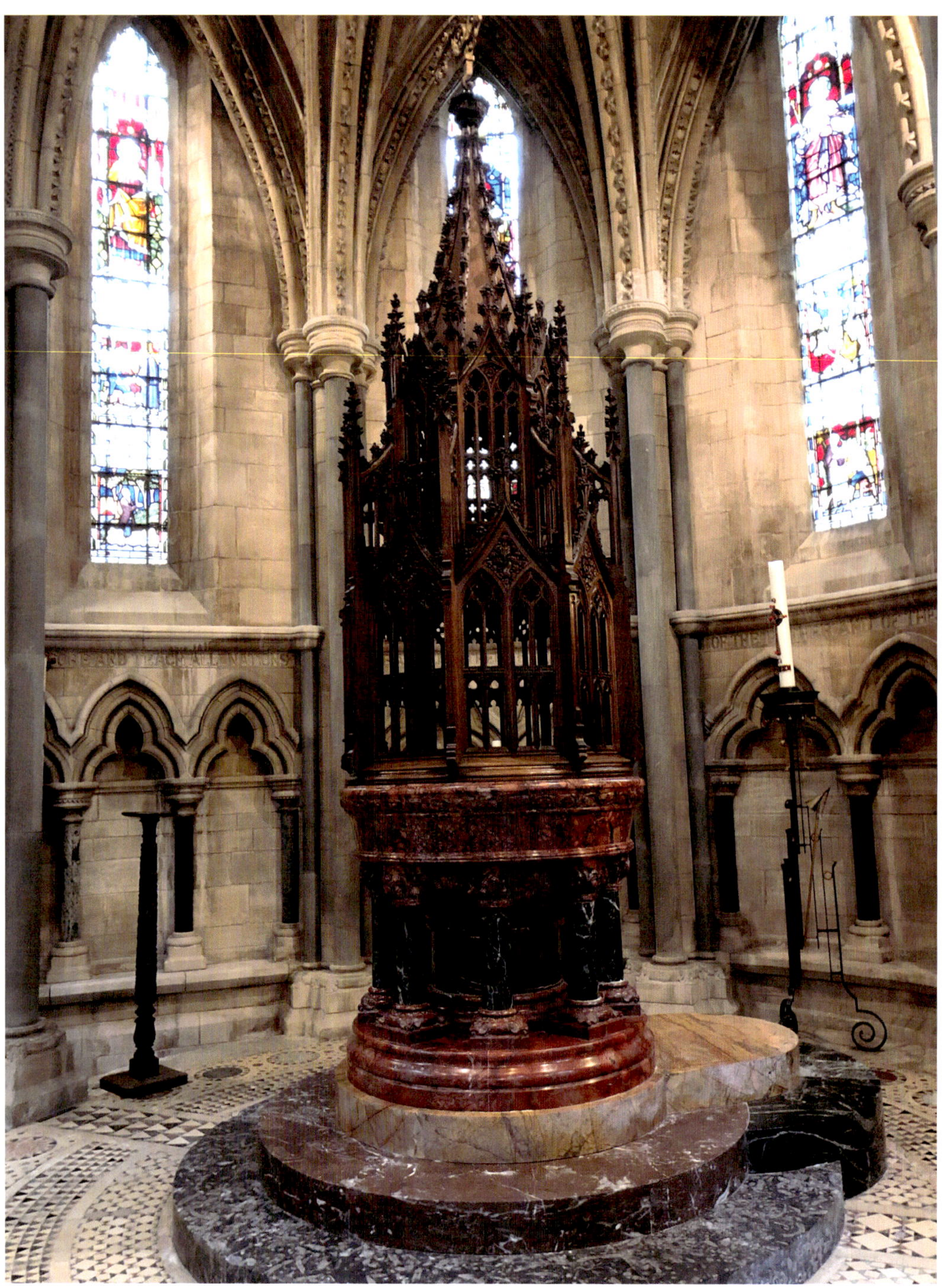

The baptistry has a red marble font that is covered by a magnificent canopy of carved oak. The windows around the circular building show scenes of the life of Truro missionary Henry Martyn.

was very clever and sent him to grammar school aged seven. By the age of sixteen Martyn was off to Cambridge, where he was fascinated by Greek and Latin, and before long he was top student for mathematics and senior wrangler. He felt that God had plans for him but worried about making provisions for his sister as his father had by now died as well. The answer to his problems came from the East India Company, who needed chaplains. Having been a curate in a rural parish in Cambridge at only twenty-one years old, he took the job to provide for Sally.

Henry endured the nine-month voyage, determined not to let seasickness stop his work as the ship's chaplain. He did not have a strong constitution, being consumptive, but he worked hard on his arrival in India. It was his mission to take the New Testament to the people, and he taught himself Persian, Hindustani, Urdu, Bengali and Arabic in order to write his translations. Henry died in Tokat, Turkey, in 1812 at only thirty-one years old. He was buried in an Armenian

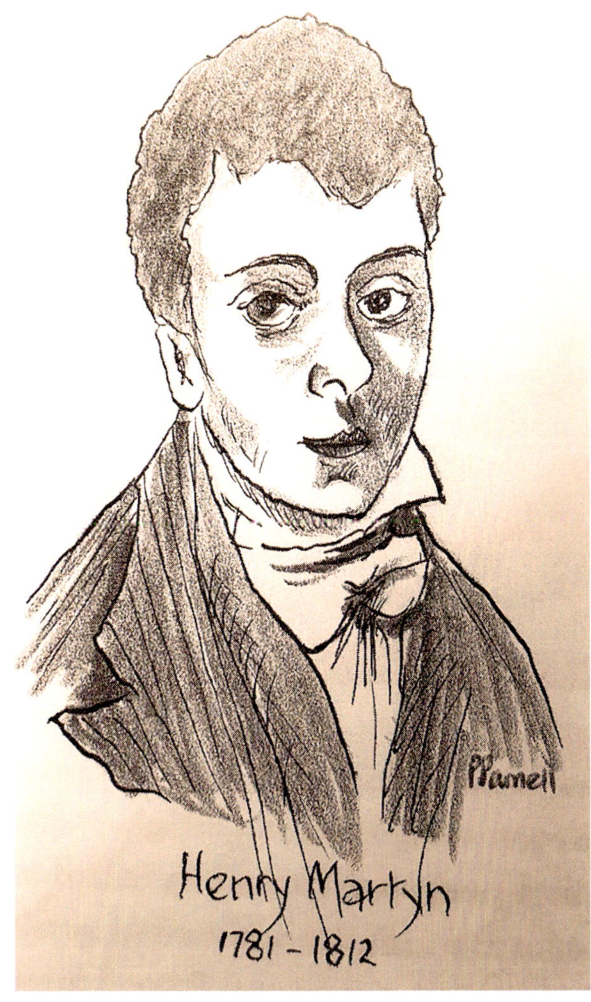

Frail Henry Martyn sailed to India, where he translated both the Book of Common Prayer and the New Testament alongside establishing a church.

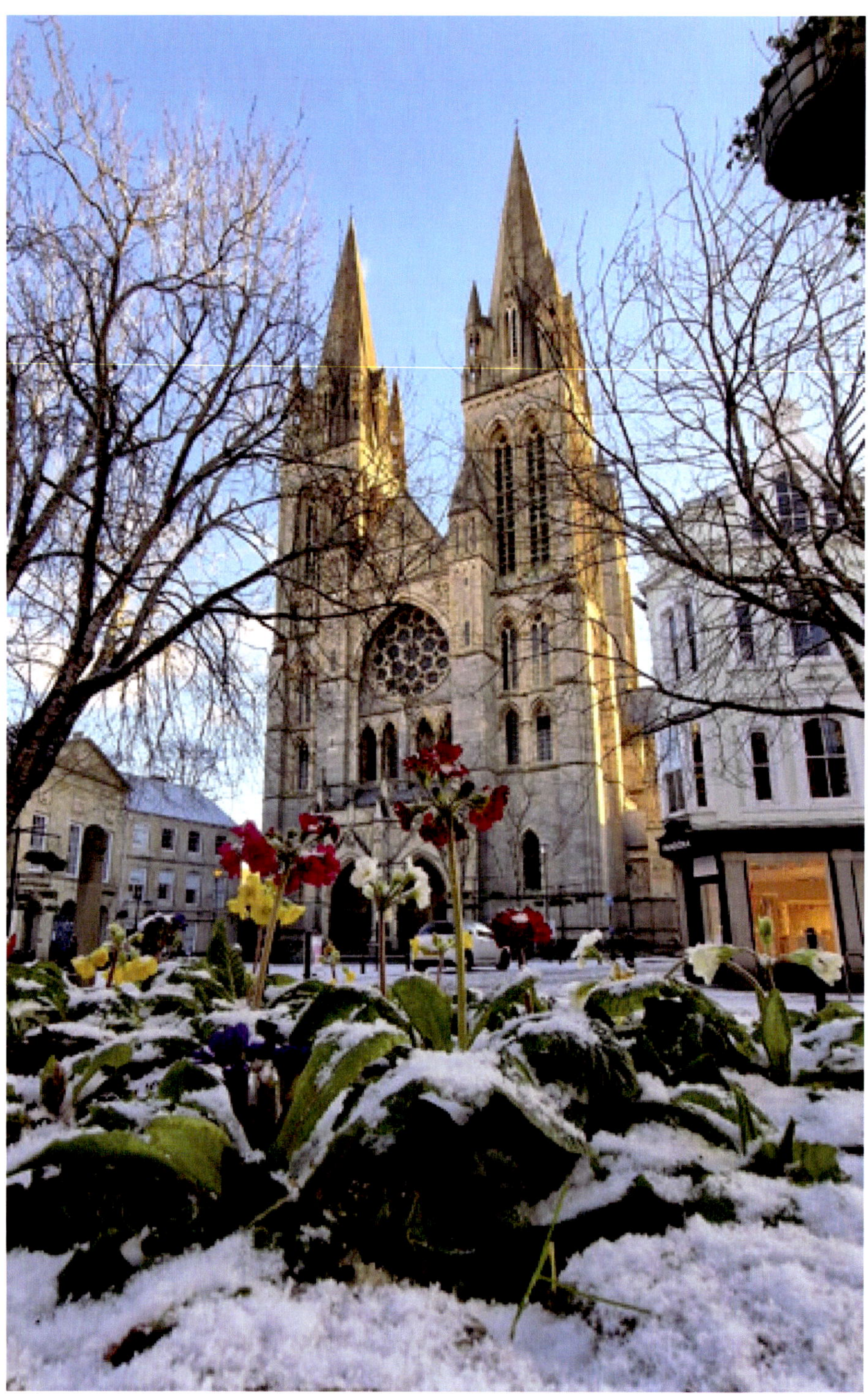

A rare snowy scene by the cathedral.

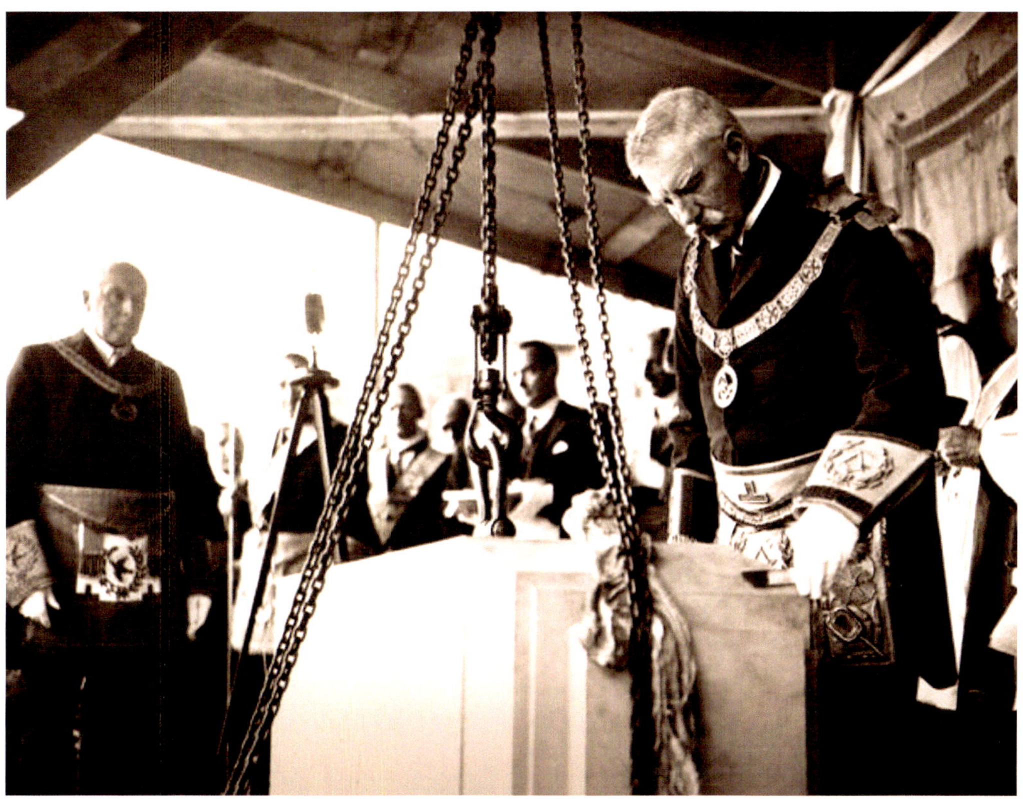

Truro dignitaries and Prince Albert wore full masonic dress when he laid the foundation stone. When dressed in his formal attire he started the trend of leaving his bottom waistcoat button undone.

cemetery near that city, having succeeded in his mission of translating the New Testament into Hindi and Persian. He had also revised an Arabic translation of the New Testament and translated the Psalter into Persian and the Book of Common Prayer into Hindi.

John Nichols Tom

An interesting but somewhat peculiar character who once resided in Pydar Street was John Nichols Tom, later to be known as 'Mad Tom'.

Tom was born in St Columb Major, and was christened in the parish church on 10 November 1799. He was the son of William Tom, landlord of the Joiners Arms. His mother, Charity Tom, was locally known as 'Cracked Charity'. Although his mother insisted on him being educated at the Bellevue Academy, established in 1800 at Penryn, it is uncertain if he did in fact attend. Some references state that he received his early education there, but Ashley Rowe writes that according to the *Bibliotheca Cornubiensis* Tom was educated only at Launceston under Dr Richard Cope.

Tom's first employment came at the age of seventeen as a clerk for Francis Camborne Paynter, a solicitor at St Columb. Three years later he left that office and decided to become landlord of a public house in Wadebridge. It was most unusual for anyone as young as twenty to be granted a licence, and this was not a successful career change because in the same year he took employment in Truro as a clerk with wine merchants Lubbock and Company. This proved more fruitful for him as he took over the business in Pydar Street when partners Plummer and Turner retired in 1827. By now he had married Catherine Fisher Fulpitt, daughter of a wealthy merchant gardener who had employed Tom as an agent in his financial affairs.

Life was looking good for the handsome young man, who stood 6 feet tall and was renowned for his strength and ability as a batsman. He grew his business to include maltings and enjoyed the company of prosperous friends.

Unfortunately for Mr Tom, things were about to take a turn for the worse. First his mother was admitted to the Cornwall Lunatic Asylum at Bodmin, then on 10 June 1828 his business premises in Pydar Street caught fire, casting much suspicion on him. Though £3,700 was paid out by the insurance company, Tom failed to continue his business and was laid low by depressive fits. Before long he set sail from Truro to Liverpool with a cargo of malt and his insurance money.

From 1830, he spent the next two years travelling to France, Greece, Turkey and Palestine. After that, a handsome bearded man dressed in flowing robes appeared in Canterbury, Kent, calling himself Sir William Percy Honeywood Courtenay, Knight of Malta and King of Jerusalem. It was, of course, John Nichols

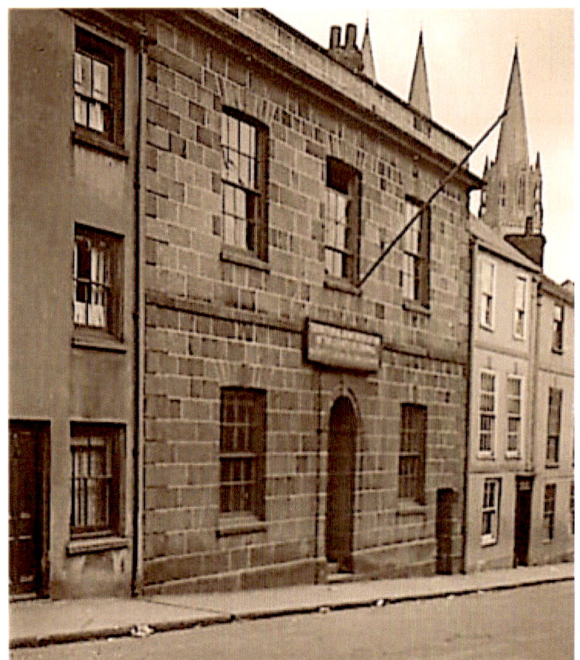

The Armoury building in Pydar Street was demolished during the first redevelopment of the area. In the early nineteenth century it was the premises of spirit merchants Plummer and Turner and this is where John Nichols Tom took on the business; the foundation stone of this building bore his initials. He was renowned for being an eccentric character with a variety of self-adopted titles.

Tom. He also claimed to be the rightful Earl of Devon and Count Rothschild and unsuccessfully contested a seat in Parliament, afterwards attacking the Customs and Excise regulations, which brought him a following among the peasantry.

His attempt to give false witness in favour of some smugglers would have seen him sentenced to transportation, but he was found to be insane and placed in a Kent lunatic asylum. His whereabouts became known to Member of Parliament Sir Hussey Vivian, who had been his neighbour in Pydar Street, and with his help Tom regained his freedom in 1837.

The following year 'Mad Tom' was up to his old tricks, proclaiming himself the Messiah and leading a mob of peasants protesting against the Poor Law. A constable was sent to arrest him but Tom shot the man dead. He then led the

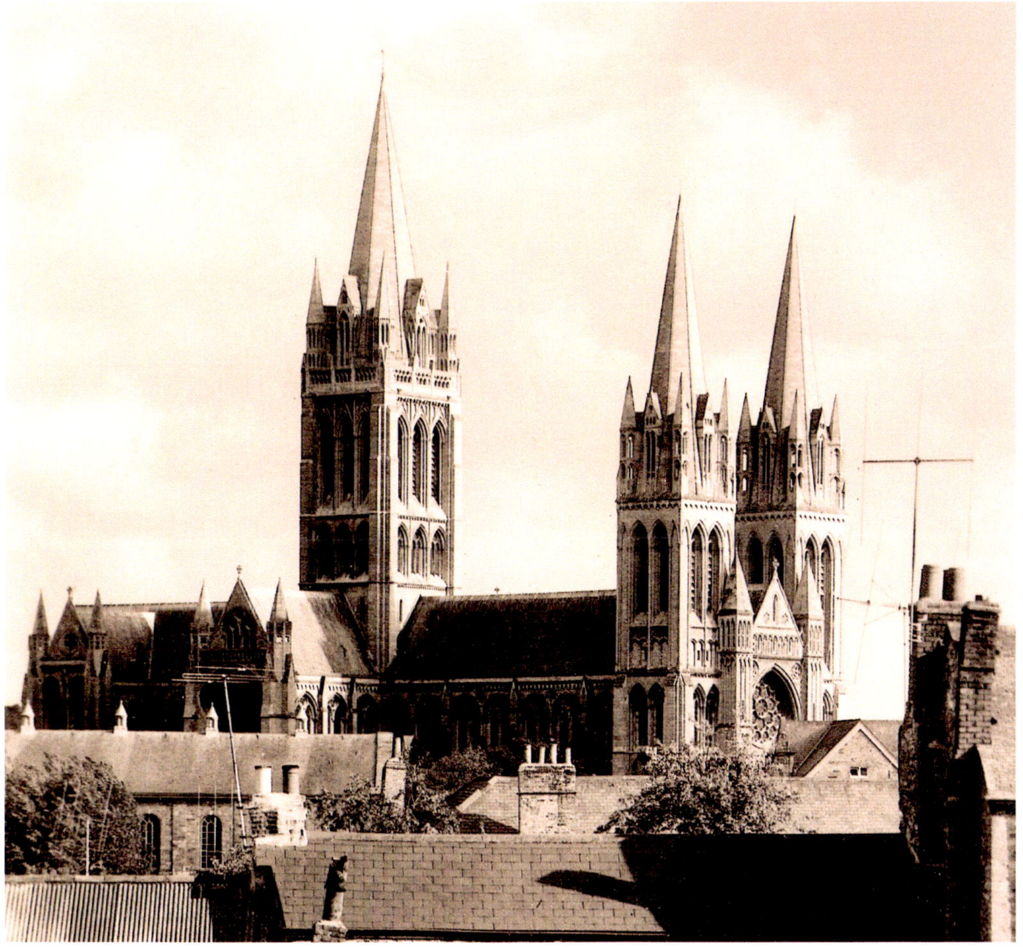

Truro Cathedral is the youngest of only three cathedrals in the United Kingdom with three spires; Lichfield Cathedral in Staffordshire and St Mary's Cathedral in Edinburgh are the other two. Lincoln Cathedral also had three spires until 1548, when the central spire collapsed.

mob into a wood where he 'administered the sacrament'. In a battle with police and the army, Tom opened fire and killed a lieutenant. Major Armstrong, the commanding officer, gave the order to fire at the mob. Nine protestors were killed, including Tom.

Tom was buried in Herne Hill, Kent after special precautions were taken against any claims to resurrection.

Ashley Rowe

A great debt of gratitude is due to Ashley Rowe, who spent much of his time researching local history and publishing his findings in the *West Briton*. Mr Rowe was born in London in 1882 and educated at Jago's School, Plymouth and later King's College London. His father was from Devon but his mother was Cornish. He embarked on a career in the Post Office in London and later was a member of the Flying Corps in the First World War. Ashley and his wife made their home in Mount Hawke, and their enthusiasm for all things Cornish saw them rewarded with the honour of becoming Cornish Bards. Many Truronians remember Ashley

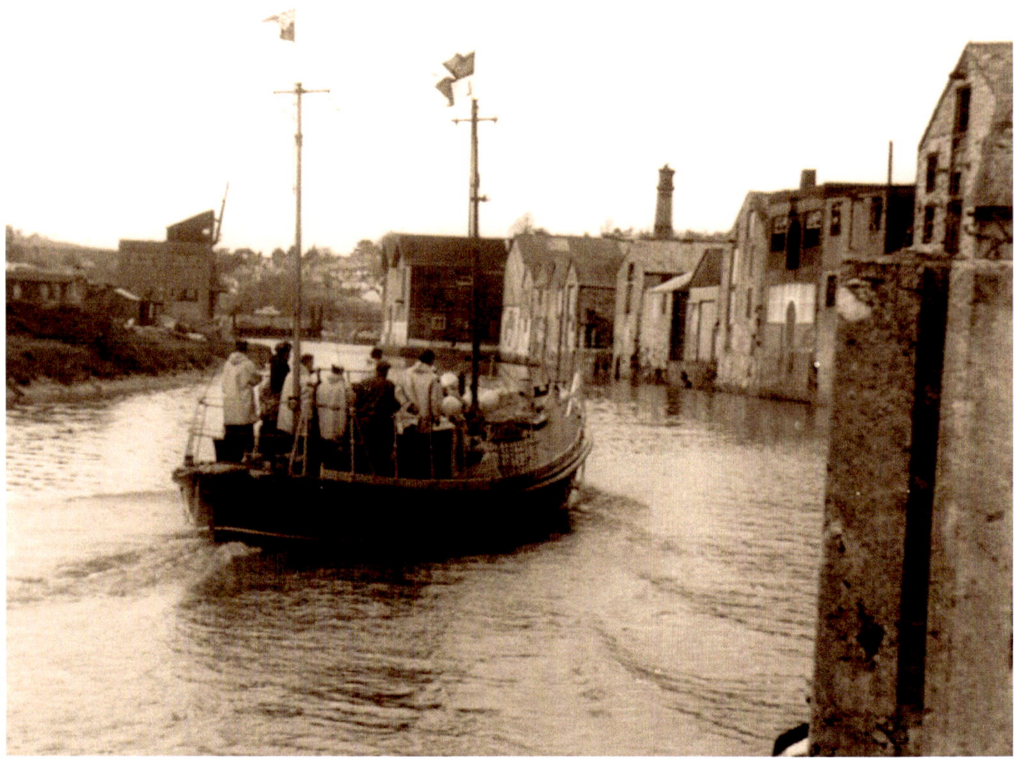

The Falmouth lifeboat on the Truro River, en route to a cathedral service in the mid-1960s. We do not know what the service was about, but we do know that the lifeboat was the *Crawford and Constance Conybeare*. The coxswain was Bert West, and Ralph Bird was also aboard.

Rowe for his weekly column in the Monday edition of the *West Briton* in which he thrilled readers with his accounts of Cornish people and events.

For twenty-three years he was the recorder for Truro Old Cornwall Society, and it was a great loss to Truro and the county when he died in 1965 at the age of eighty-two. The following are two suitably quirky extracts from his columns, the first one being from a paper he read to the Royal Institution of Cornwall.

In 1843 Queen Victoria and Prince Albert were on a cruise when news arrived in the county that it was likely that the Queen would honour Falmouth with a call. The local dignitaries were able to pay their respects with ease but councillors from Truro went down to Falmouth on the steamship *Dart* as ordinary sightseers. The Mayor of Truro Mr Lamb waited for the address that he hoped to give to be completed and set off for Falmouth in his own coach. When he arrived he realised that the Mayors of both Falmouth and Penryn had dressed in their regalia and were in barges, but he did not have his mayoral robes or maces with him. He set off in a small boat to join the others but then chaos ensued as the little boat sank beneath the water. Luckily, he could swim but he was soaked as was the gown belonging to an ex-mayor that he had been lent. It is not known whether it was announced that the Mayor of Truro was on the water or in the water but the Queen seemed satisfied. As for the spectators, they thought it was all very amusing, as did the Mayor himself.

...

It turned out to be a memorable occasion on 7 September 1846, the day of Truro Annual Sailing and Rowing Match, when royalty visited Truro. A visit from Prince Albert caused excitement when he visited the town. Queen Victoria was on her yacht *Victoria and Albert* in Falmouth but she decided it would be interesting to go up the Fal on *Fairy*, her smaller boat. The cannon was fired for the start of the most important race just as *Fairy* came up the river. The water was full of boats but the committee boat with the umpires on board managed to clear a path for *Fairy* so that there was no inconvenience to the Queen and five-year-old Duke of Cornwall. The committee members were so delighted that they completely forgot the race they were monitoring. After that day Edmund Turner M P announced that the Queen had agreed that the races were to be styled 'Truro Royal Regatta'.

Weird or What?

The Green

The Truro River has played an important part in Truro's industry, not only for shipping but also for oystering, recreational entertainment and much more.

A good living was made by the people of St Clement, who pickled oysters and sent them in quart barrels to the West Indies. The fish-and-oyster women sold their stock in cloister-styled buildings once known as Middle Row, located in what we presently know as Boscawen Street. When pavements were dug up in the area, huge quantities of oyster shells were revealed.

For hundreds of years the channel between Truro and Malpas had been silting up, and this had great effect on the size of the ships able to pass through. In 1701

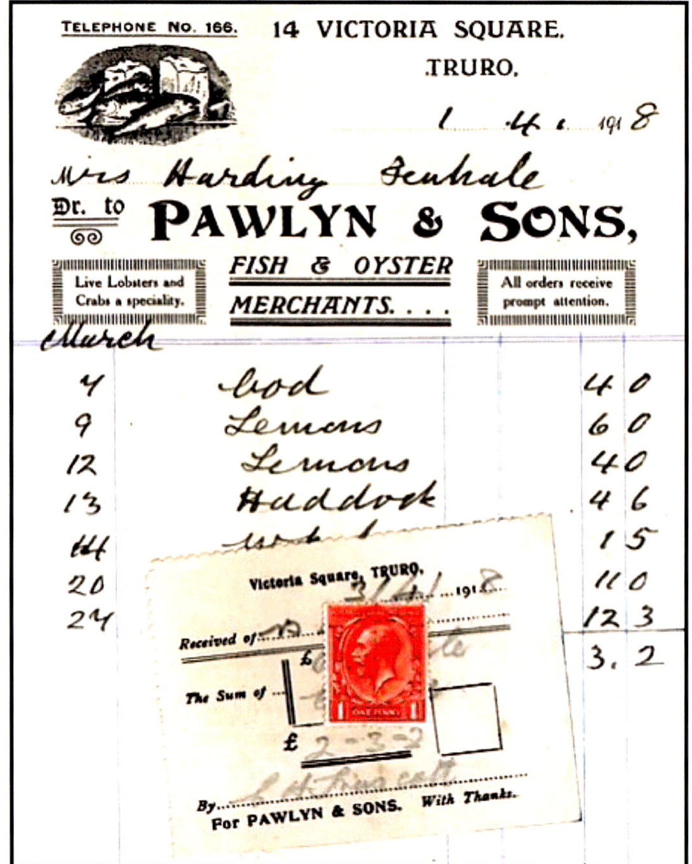

Pawlyn Fish Merchants' billhead in 1918, showing oysters were still available to order for those who could afford them.

it was recorded in the Borough Order Book that 'it was difficult for vessels of usuall burthen to come upp the river for the channel and river beginns to be choakt'. The river mud was a subject of much debate over many decades, with various suggestions made for dealing with the 'accursed mud'. Throughout the nineteenth century, Messrs Rowe erected a kiln on the river near The Parade so that they might bake the mud into bricks, but on exposure to moisture the bricks simply returned to mud. Other attempts were made by Mr Radford in 1877 and by Harveys in 1892. It was unclear whether they were more successful than Mr Rowe, but those living nearby complained about the noxious fumes from the kilns, which killed off plants in their gardens.

As far back as 1642, the old folk of Truro would talk about the land reclaimed from the sea that we now know as The Green, next to the Town Quay. Over the years this area has been an important and active part of Truro, with locals taking pride in its port status. Indeed, it had its own customs house known as Green House, situated on Back Quay, where the Royal Arms faced out onto The Green. Sadly, in 1882, when Truro lost its customs house, The Green lost its status as a port and was reduced to a creek.

The area was first known as The Bowling Green in 1680, because this was its original purpose – it was a place for the grammar school boys to relax and

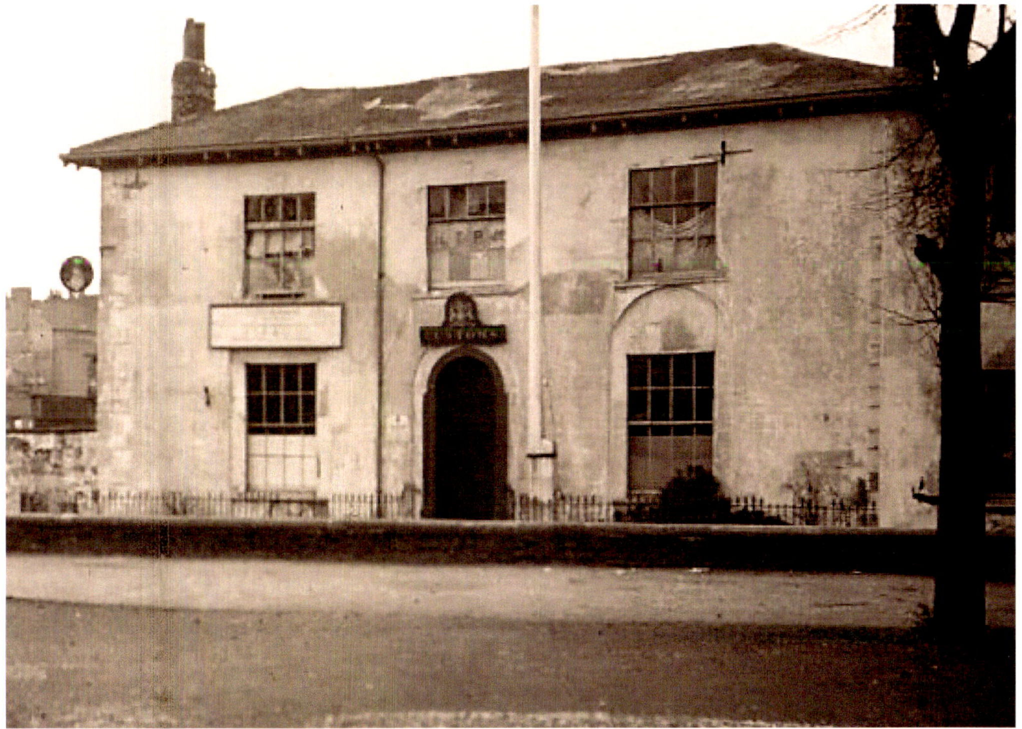

Green House faced the river and was the place where dues were paid for the use of the busy port until it was demoted to a creek.

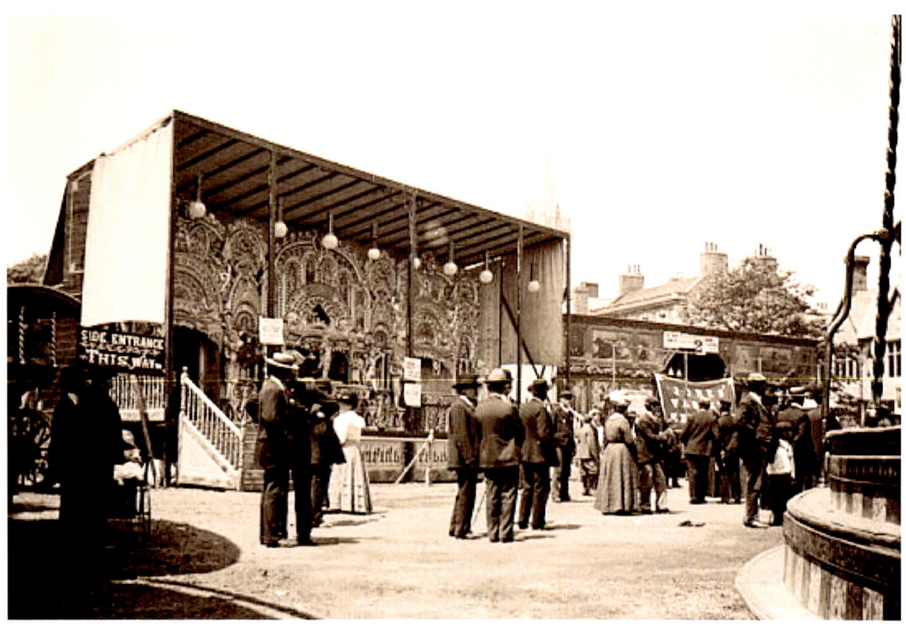

For many years various travelling fairs would set up on The Green for their annual visit to Truro.

play. On occasions the turf got damaged by local people wearing pattens over their shoes; this was unwelcome news to the town clerk, who offered a reward for information about trespassers on the site. It enjoyed other purposes, too, hosting public announcements by the local MP and being the site of fairs and promenades.

Although the area was well used, the Town Quay and Bowling Green were frequently flooded and their condition was often complained about. Consequently, in 1728 ramparts were built around them but this did little to help. In need of money for repairs, the town clerk asked for help from Lord Falmouth. He gratefully returned with £300 for to improve the area; he had enough to also fund the building of a wall around the new prison. The level of the Bowling Green and Town Quay was raised again in 1888, and later still 2,000 tons of rubbish was placed atop the old surface. This brought sixty or more people to the area, who searched through the rubbish looking for coins, jewellery or any other finds that had been lost or thrown away over the years. In 1899, stables that had been on the site were demolished, providing more space for a forthcoming Whitsun Fair. In a mocking tone, locals now called it 'The Invisible Green'.

Suggestions were made for the surface to be metalled, and in 1915, after yet another layer of ashes had been laid, this was done. However, now the locals were unhappy because their favourite promenade was now lost forever. The area is now home to the Truro bus station, and so continues to enjoy constant traffic.

Weather

Truro has been visited by some strange weather. In 1755 the vicar of Kea recorded in the parish register a report of a tsunami wave that came up the Truro River as far as Ladock.

Decades later, on Christmas Day 1803, Truro was in the throes of a terrible gale thought by most people to be the worst that the town had ever experienced. However, worse was to come in just a few days. Two houses on Lemon Street were damaged when a new wall was blown over, taking with it the roof of the second house along with one of its walls. Also lost were the roof of the stables at the barracks and much of a wall, leading to comments about the build quality.

On 5 October 1858, during the celebration of the St Kea Feast – which also marked the opening of a new church – it was noted that the tail of Donati's Comet was visible. Twelve months later three great tidal waves were documented, one of which came up the Truro River; the waves were then thought to have been caused by submarine earthquakes. Later in the same month, the effect of an earthquake was felt in Malpas and the surrounding areas of Truro. A few days later a hurricane and torrents of rain occurred in the same areas. Unfortunately, at Wheal Prosper mine in Chacewater a fifteen-year-old girl named Emily Williams

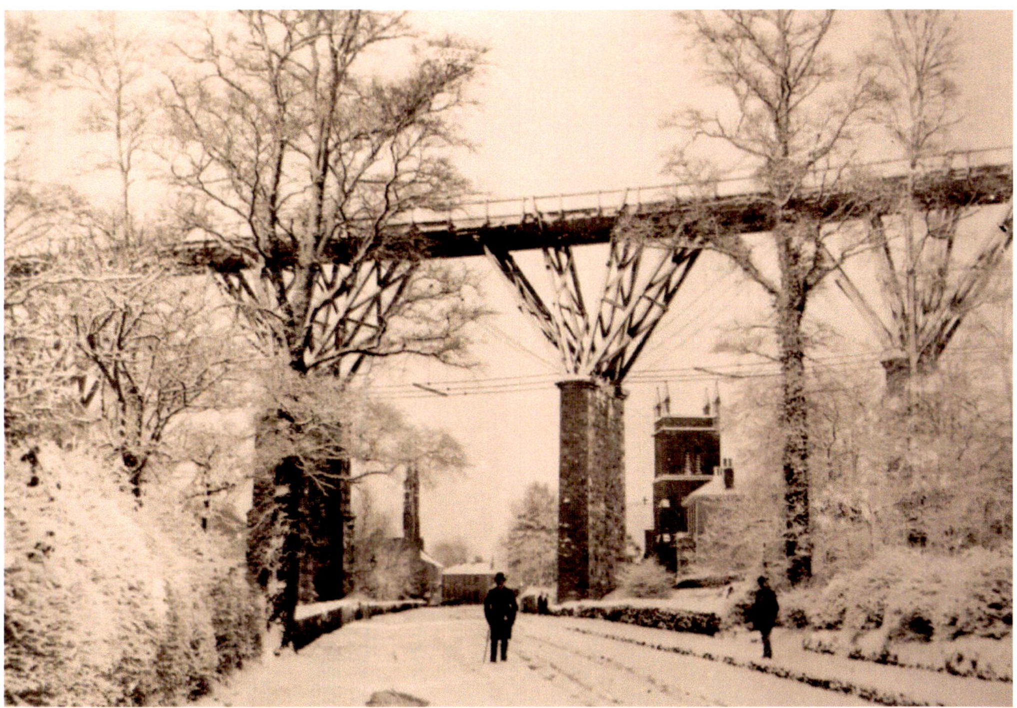

This snowy scene at Carvedras Viaduct in St George's Road shows the power lines that became entangled with branches of fallen trees during one of the severe storms of the late nineteenth century.

was drowned while crossing a stream. During this time the extreme weather conditions caused several fatal wrecks around the Cornish coast.

This period of severe weather continued in 1860 with frightening thunder and lightning storms causing another tragic fatality when Betsy Jewell of Philleigh was struck by lightning.

Kenwyn Church suffered some damage when lightning struck the south-west pinnacle of the tower, causing it to fall to the ground. Other property in the area was damaged, including a bullock shed, but fortunately the animals were unhurt. There were also reports during this month relating to the shock of an earthquake felt in the town around the Lemon Street area as well as on Rosewin Row where doors opened and closed on their own. People were so frightened that they jumped out of bed and ran into the street screaming. Then, in 1864, there was a drought that stretched almost uninterrupted from April to August.

The *West Briton* had further news of extreme weather for the residents of Truro when in October 1877 it reported a terrific hurricane had raged through the city. It started on Sunday evening around 6 p.m. and increased in violence, with hurricane-force winds reaching their peak by midnight.

The next morning the townspeople awoke to inspect the damage that the storm had caused. A very large tree in St George's Road had fallen and landed across the river. Its large branches had tangled with overhead telegraph wires and bent the poles that had been carrying them. Nearby the St George's School bell turret had been carried away. There were many reports of fallen slates and tiles and parts of the Town Quay were nearly blown into the water. Other residents were alarmed to find their chimneypots smashed to the ground and panes of glass broken. One Mr Salmon was dismayed to find his vinery had been destroyed, the vines having been blown away. Even the town clock was stopped by the punishing winds. The list of damages was endless. The noise and fright of the storm terrified a woman from Richmond Hill so much that it caused her to run to the police station for help. Nor did the storm show any mercy to the town clergy. The chimney on the house belonging to Reverend Finnemore fell on the roof of Reverend Fuller's home, smashing through to the bedroom where a child lay sleeping. Some of the bricks fell into the child's bed, but the occupants escaped unharmed.

Many years later, the *West Briton* was to report yet another occurrence of extreme weather. During the summer of 1936, a freak thunderstorm broke over Truro. Although it only lasted for fifteen minutes, it brought chaos to certain parts of the city, centred on Calenick Street and Lemon Street. On a Saturday at midday the sky darkened, and there was a sudden downpour of rain with hailstones as big as marbles that carpeted the ground.

Neighbours Mrs Stevenson and Mrs Lean were standing in their doorways in Calenick Street remarking on the rainwater pouring down the passageway between their houses when suddenly they were startled by a thunderous noise. Flames shot through the passage and they were thrown with force into their kitchens. Smoke belched out of the houses, and once it cleared the damage done

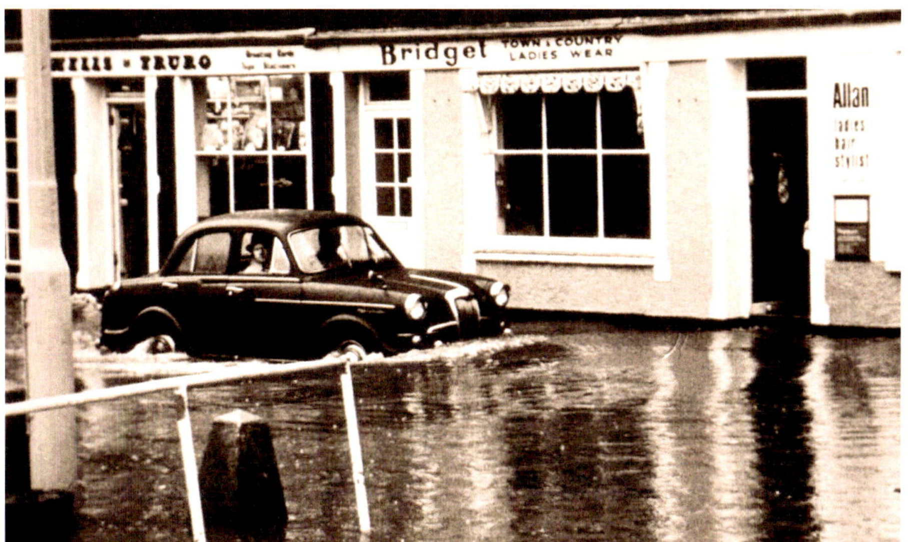

Above: Over the decades Truro has suffered from flooding throughout the town. In past years a warning was given by the old air-raid siren. Here we have Old Bridge Street, which was often flooded, in 1962.

Right: This pretty snowy scene in The Leats shows a lady and her dog trudging through the snow.

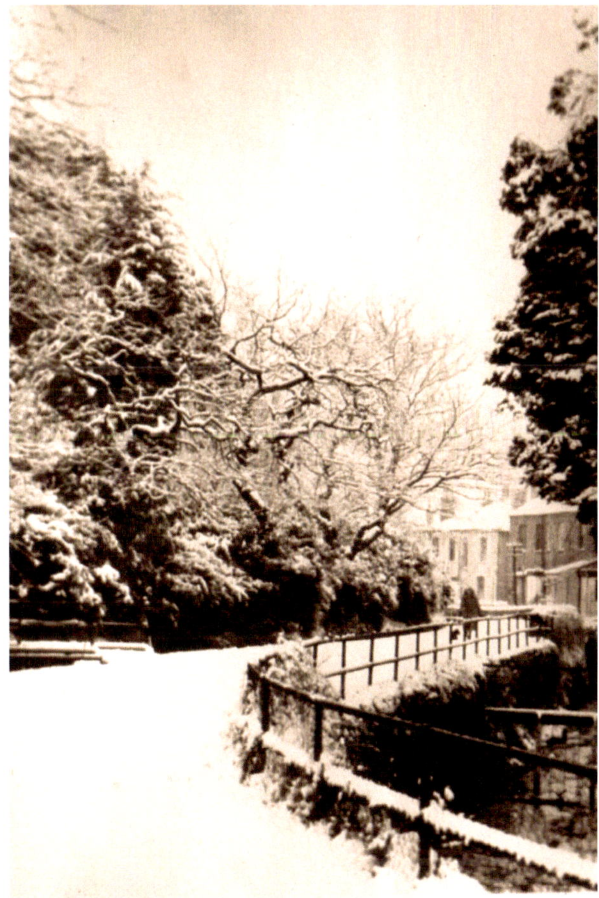

to both homes was plain to see. Even their wireless sets were put out of action. Both ladies related their terrifying stories to the *West Briton*.

People in Lemon Street saw both the tremendous lightning and the Calenick Street fireball looming over the rooftops and rushed to take shelter in the Plaza Cinema. Mr Grose, secretary of the Truro Cricket Club, was about to make a telephone call when the receiver was dashed from his hand by the force of the storm and he was thrown some distance. A torrent of rainwater also choked the town's gutters and drains, causing flooding throughout Chapel Hill and Kenwyn Street.

Skating at Pencalenick

In 1798, John Macadam (later renowned for building roads with a smooth, hard surface) decided to experiment with using Cornish stone for his roads, building a new turnpike road from the Truro workhouse on Tregolls Road to Kiggon that is part of the A39 today. The road later provided a route to Kiggon Pond, which was created on the Pencalenick Estate in the 1820s by estate owner John Vivian. This was achieved by damming off part of the Tresillian River. In 1853, when Vivian's widow wanted to sell the estate, it transpired that the bed of the lake was actually

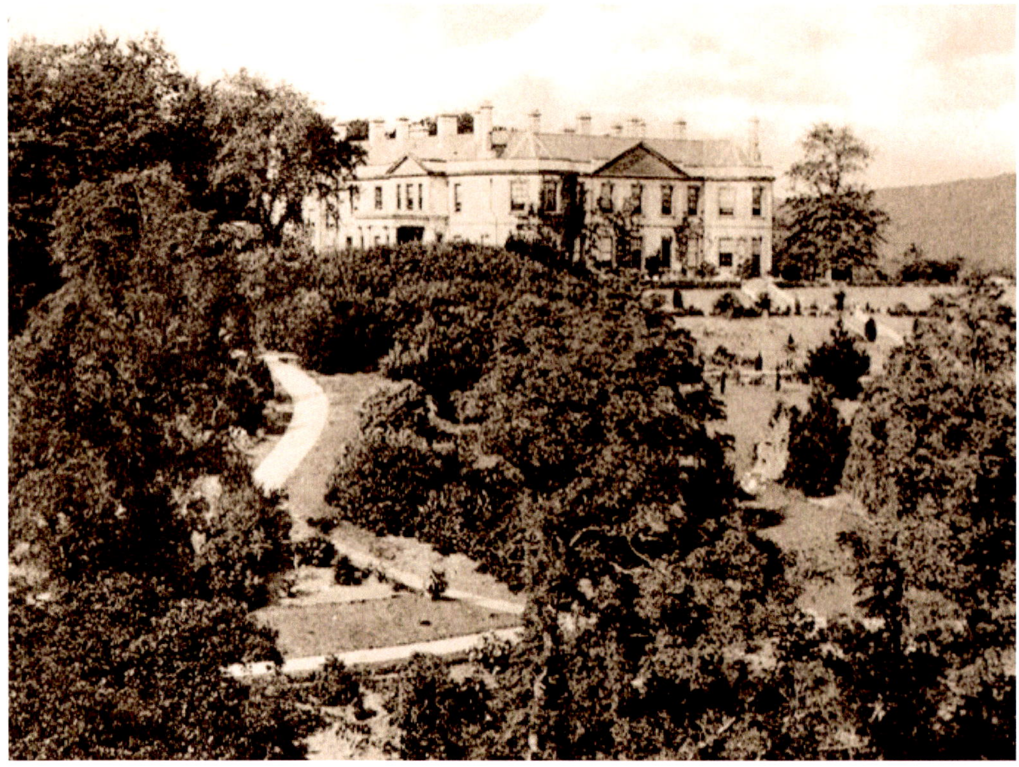

The grand Pencalenick House, set on high ground surrounded by woodland, was once home to the wealthy Williams family. For many years it has been Pencalenick School.

the foreshore of the Tresillian River and belonged to the Duchy of Cornwall. Not wanting to lose the lake, she purchased the foreshore from the duchy. Over the years the pond was often frozen over in winter, which encouraged local people to skate there.

According to the *Cornwall Gazette* of 15 January 1891, a fatal incident took place on the pond. On a Sunday afternoon, when almost 100 skaters were having fun on the deceptively thin ice, it gave way. Three men of Truro fell into the icy water. They were Sgt Teeling, a recruiting officer; Alfred Islip, a manager of the International Tea Company; and S. G. Thomson, a dentist's assistant to Mr Toope. At first some of the onlookers thought the incident was harmless and amusing, but it soon became clear that this was serious. Realising the danger, people scrambled to help, bringing over a gate, rope and ladders.

Islip and Teeling were both light and small men, so they managed to clamber out of the water with some help. They were exhausted but later managed to walk home. Thomson, however, though a good swimmer, struggled to keep himself afloat in the freezing water. Two brave young men, a blacksmith named Keast and a tool sharpener called Burrows, tried to reach the drowning man but all three disappeared under the icy water. Two other young men named May and Allen pushed a gate towards the drowning men, but Allen fell into the water and was pulled out unconscious. Thomson hung onto the gate, which kept his head above the water while he encouraged the other two men to stay afloat. Sadly, Keast sank and drowned, and a little later Burrows gave up the fight and slipped beneath the surface. May threw a rope to Thomson, and after several attempts he caught it and tied it around his waist and was pulled to safety. Thomson and Allen were taken to Pencalenick Mansion, the home of the Williams family, where they were treated with the utmost care and kindness. By order of Michael Henry Williams, Dr King of Truro attended both men and by evening they had recovered sufficiently to go home.

The boat fetched from St Clement to retrieve the bodies of Keast and Burrows was holed, so another boat was fetched to return the corpses to the shore. After that, the bodies of these brave men were finally taken to their homes on a cart.

Ski Slope

For a part of the country with a temperate climate, the people of Truro seemed to have a passion for ice skating. In the early 1900s, the county ice rink in the City Hall would be a popular place to meet friends and have fun. The museum holds a photograph of the skating rink's cafe *circa* 1910, with ladies enjoying their tea and being waited on by a maid.

In 2006, as part of the Christmas celebrations, an ice ski slope was built on the piazza, a very unusual sight in Truro. Young children were safely strapped into a toboggan before being pulled to the top and allowed to slide gently down. Adults also had an enjoyable time on it. Several times since then an outdoor rink has been set up in the grounds of the cathedral, allowing people to have some winter fun.

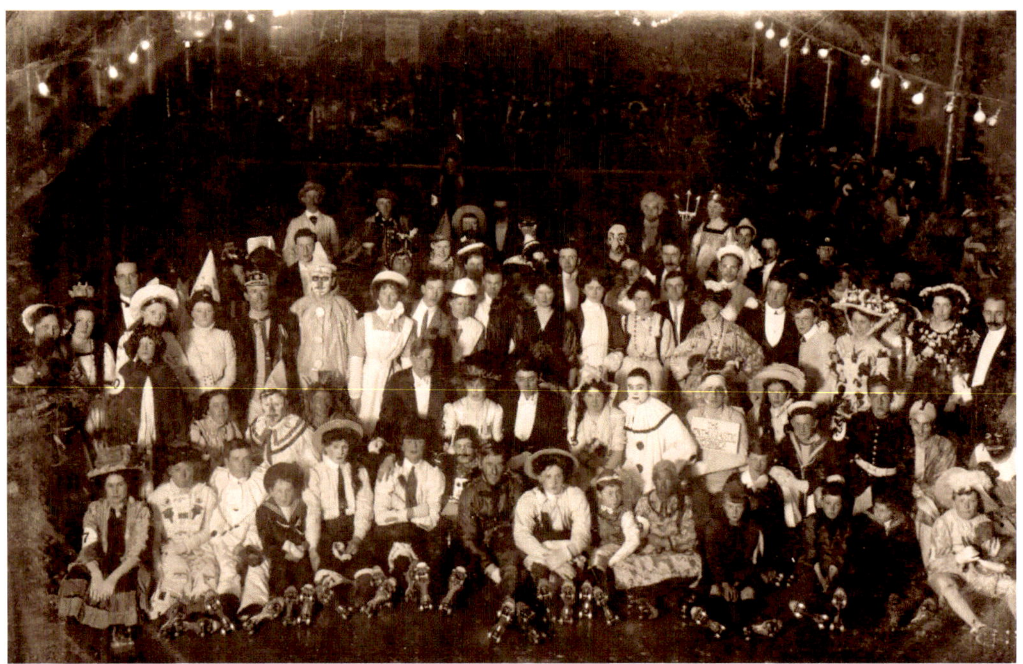

The county skating rink in Truro City Hall was the venue for a fancy-dress carnival on Easter Monday 1910.

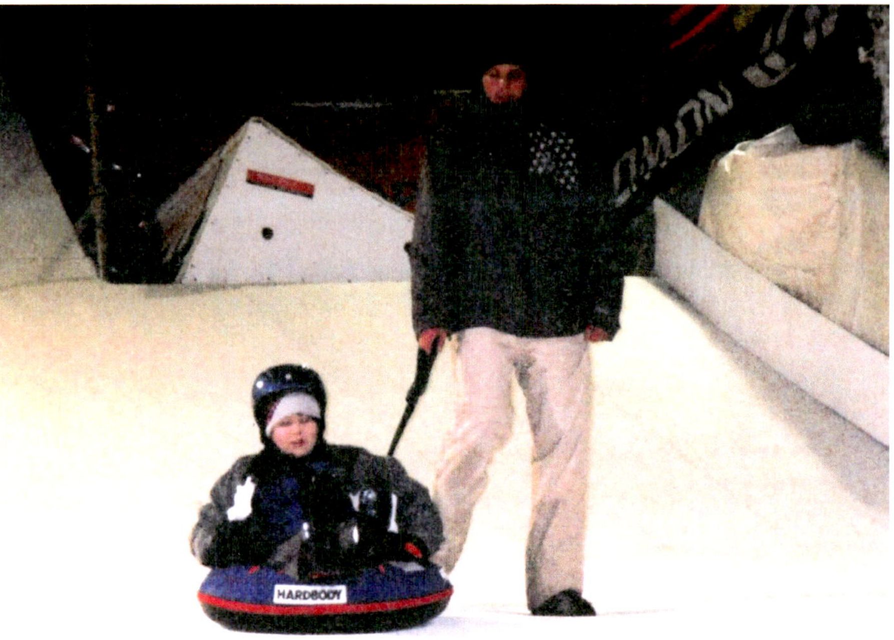

In 2006, a ski slope was constructed on the piazza as a seasonal treat. People were happy to queue in the freezing weather for their turn.

Lost Cap

Another story, reported as 'Plucky Rescue' in the *West Briton* on 24 October 1907, concerned a young deaf boy. He had been with a number of other children playing in a field near the Malpas Road Quarry on Saturday afternoon when he lost his cap, which lodged itself halfway down the highest part of the quarry. Not wanting to go home without it, or indeed realising the danger, he tried to retrieve it by climbing up from the bottom. Once he had reached his cap, he tried to climb to the top but the ground began to give way beneath his feet. He soon realised he was unable to move up or down. Luckily for the boy, the Reverend Baker and his wife happened to be passing by and noticed the lad was in danger of falling. At once Mr Baker ran to Mr Edwards' store in Malpas Road for assistance. Eight or more men arrived with a quantity of rope but could not reach the unfortunate boy. Then they went back to the shop and returned with one of their longest ladders, but still it was to no avail. It was now necessary for someone to climb further to rescue him. Attempts to reach the boy were made by several men, but each time the scree gave way beneath their feet. Eventually, with brave perseverance, one of the men was able to get close enough to hold on to the frightened boy. Thankfully, man, boy and cap were then safely brought to the ground.

Pencalenick Obelisk

Pencalenick House has an intriguing and fascinating history to tell. Just a few miles from Truro, at present it is a special school, situated in a relatively secluded estate surrounded by woodland. The building was constructed in 1881 by Mr Michael H. Williams, who purchased the Pencalenick Estate in 1879 from the Vivian family, and so became the owner of 100 acres of land and a Georgian house.

The wealthy Mr Williams, related to the Williams family of mine owners, smelters and merchant bankers, demolished the old Georgian house and built the much grander Pencalenick House, which was set on high ground surrounded by woodland and overlooked the new Italian gardens, with views of the Tresillian River.

Near to Pencalenick School, and within the woodland, is a mysterious obelisk that is approximately 35 feet high and sits on solid blocks of granite. The enigma of this stone structure is that there is no inscription of who erected it or why in this secluded area. Many people travelling along the busy Truro–Tresillian road nearby may never know of its existence, but various people have researched the history of the monument and published their findings, with two possible stories for its origin.

One theory is that it is a memorial to Woodcock, a much-loved and famous old stagecoach horse that travelled the road between Tresillian and Truro. Sadly, on a sharp bend on this road Woodcock dropped dead. Since then the area has been known as Woodcock Corner. Woodcock was owned by the Vivian family, so the Pencalenick Obelisk was possibly erected in Woodcock's memory.

Another story, told by Mr Francis T. Williams to the *West Briton*, states that Mr Vivian was once standing in front of his fireplace when the floor beneath him gave way, and he quickly grabbed hold of the mantlepiece, saving himself from

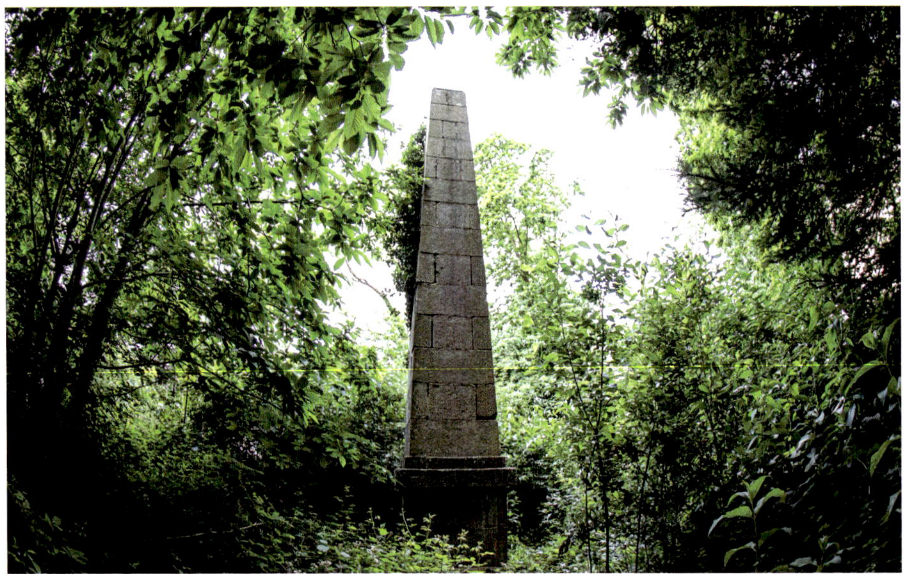

The true origin of the Pencalenick obelisk remains a mystery.

injury or falling into the cellar below. It is believed there was an old mineshaft beneath the foundations of the house, and the obelisk was said to be a reminder of lucky escape from injury or death. This theory also mentions that there is a tablet to his memory in St Clement Church.

In the *West Briton* in 1967, Mr Penhallurick, who was then curator of the Royal Institution of Cornwall, wrote that the earliest reference he could find was on a 1908 Ordnance Survey map where it was simply marked as 'Obelisk'.

The monument remains a quirky mystery.

Devil's Arch Bridge

A short distance from Pencalenick House is the Devil's Arch Bridge, part of the old driveway to the Pencalenick Estate. Legend has it that it is one of the most haunted places in the area.

When travelling from Tresillian, this road is often used as a shortcut to Truro, despite its very narrow passing places and the necessity of braving the forbidding Devil's Arch Bridge.

There are many sinister stories about the bridge that most local people know, and whether you are driving or walking under it, it sends a chill down your spine. Spooky stories include that of a highwayman who would dangle a noose from the top of the bridge to hang passing horsemen or coach drivers before stealing their belongings.

Then there is the ghost of a man on horseback, complete with spectral coach and horses, and people in Victorian dress and a lady in a white dress and bonnet. The sound of invisible galloping horses has also been heard going up the road, and if this doesn't frighten readers, the thought of the devil sitting on the bridge at night, waiting to possess your soul, should be enough for most to hold their breath as they dare to traverse it. By night or day, it is said, sounding your horn and flashing your car lights is a must to safely pass beneath.

There has even been a quirky story that the ghosts of Royalist soldiers have been spotted there. This would make sense, as it was at nearby Tresillian Bridge in 1646 that Sir Ralph Hopton, leader of the Cornish Royalist Army, surrendered to Sir Thomas Fairfax, commander of Cromwell's New Model Army.

Regardless, if you are driving a large or tall vehicle it is definitely much safer to keep to the main road than to chance getting stuck under this low bridge!

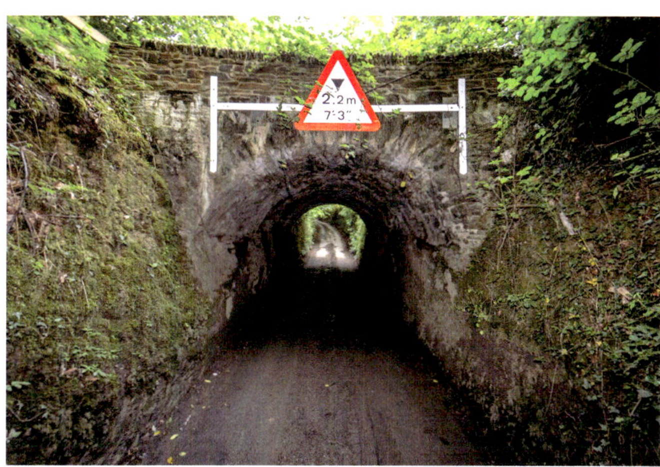

Right: The spooky Devil's Arch Bridge on the approach from Truro looks quite scary even in daylight.

Below: The Tresillian side of the Devil's Arch Bridge is a well-used shortcut to Truro by day but often avoided late at night.

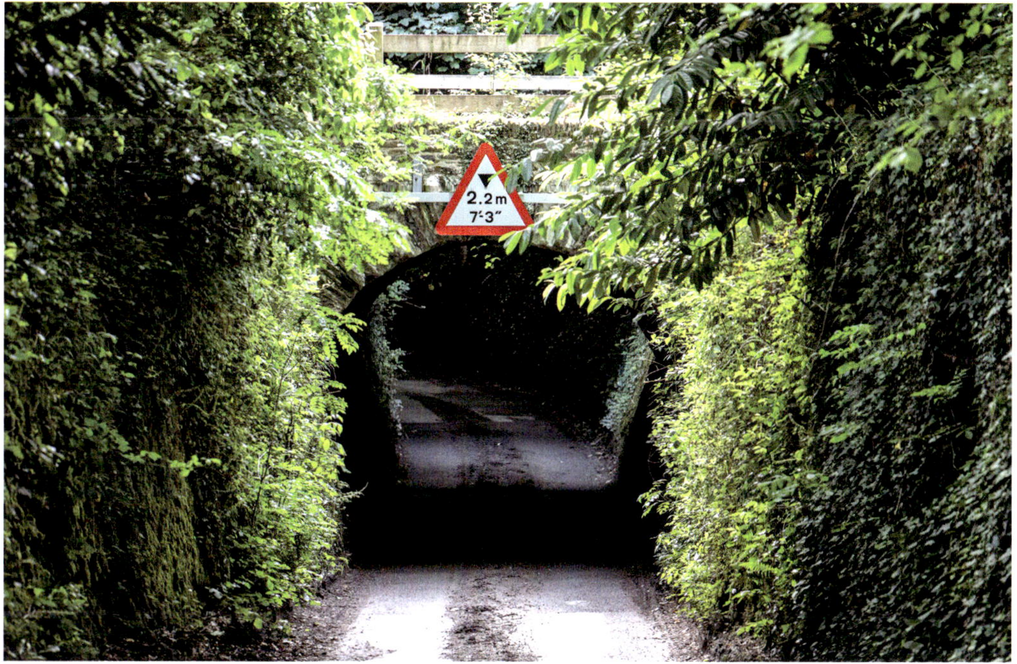

Legends and Laughter

Crossing Place

Malpas, meaning bad passage (correctly pronounced Mopus), has a fascinating Celtic legend which dates back to the sixth century.

King Mark of Cornwall, it is said, sent his nephew Tristan to Ireland to escort his future bride, Princess Iseult, to Cornwall. During the journey they accidentally drank a potion and fell passionately in love. King Mark felt angry and betrayed, so in their attempts to escape him they hid in the forest of Moresk before crossing the river at La Mal Pas, the early name for Malpas.

Jenny Mopus was the nickname of a woman called Jane Davies. She was a big, strong person who rowed the ferryboat *Happy Go Lucky* over the river at Malpas in the early nineteenth century. Cheerful passengers were often taken

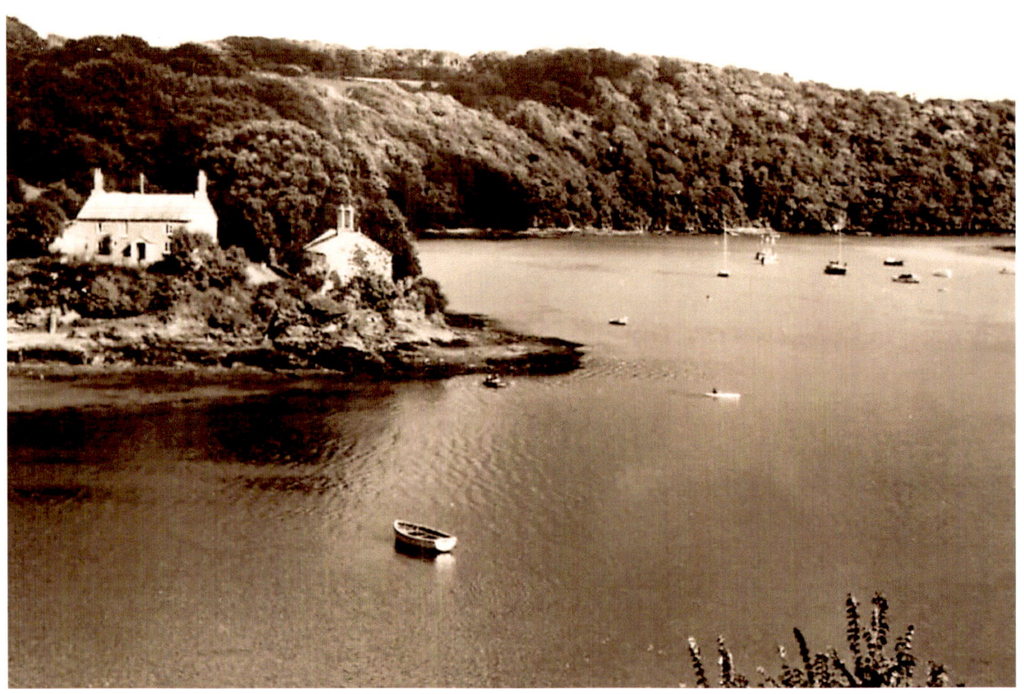

According to legend, this is the place at Malpas where Tristan and Iseult crossed the river to escape from King Mark.

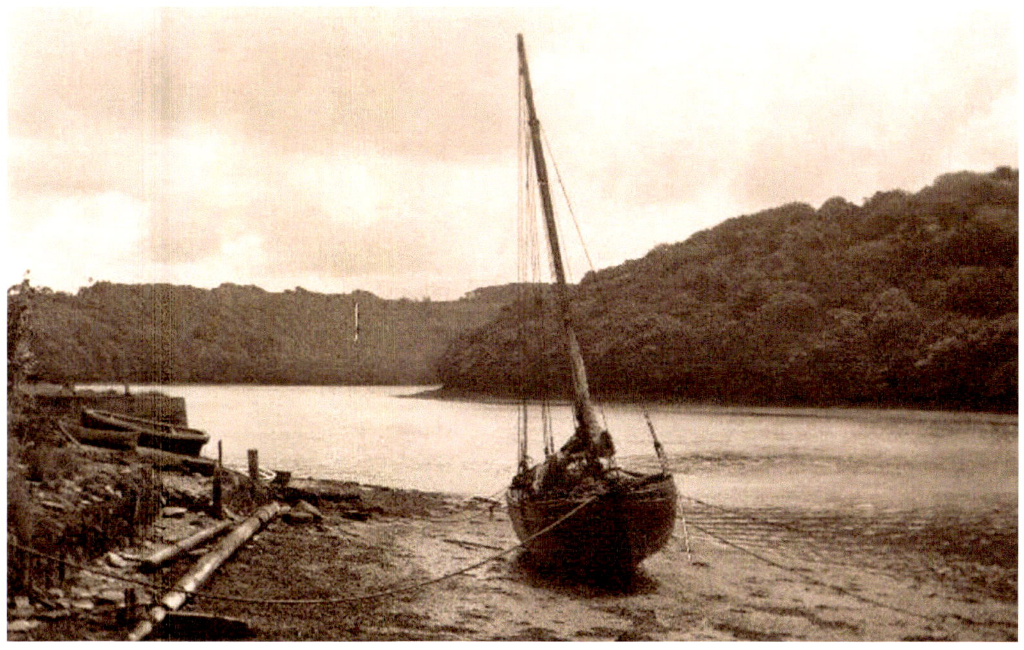

A serene scene at Malpas in bygone days.

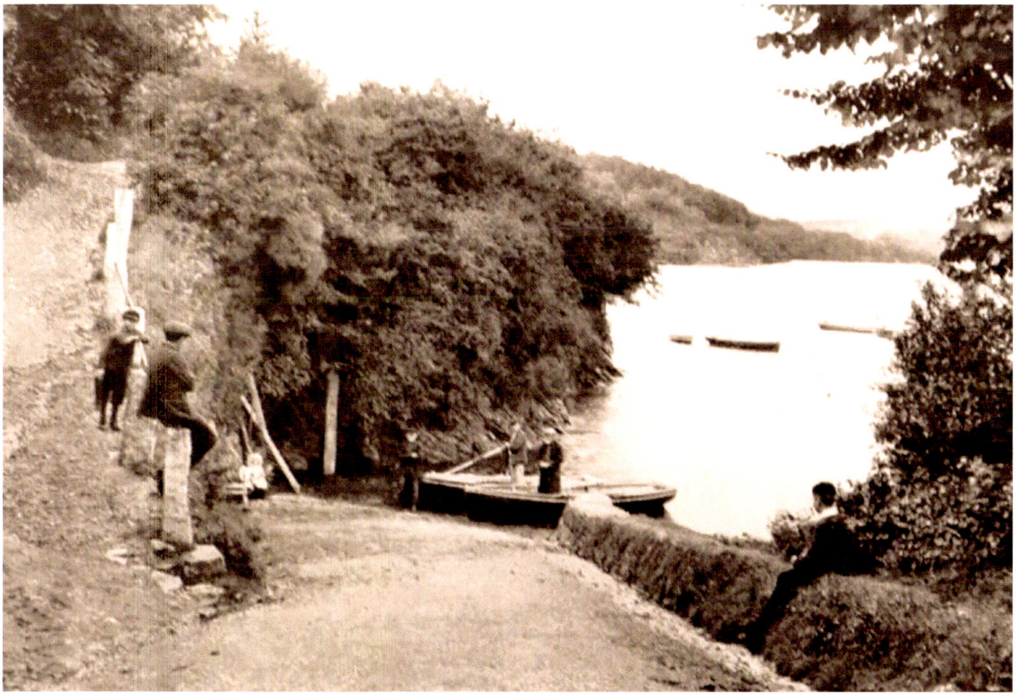

Here we see the Truro side of the boat ferry that has been well used since the days of Jenny Mopus.

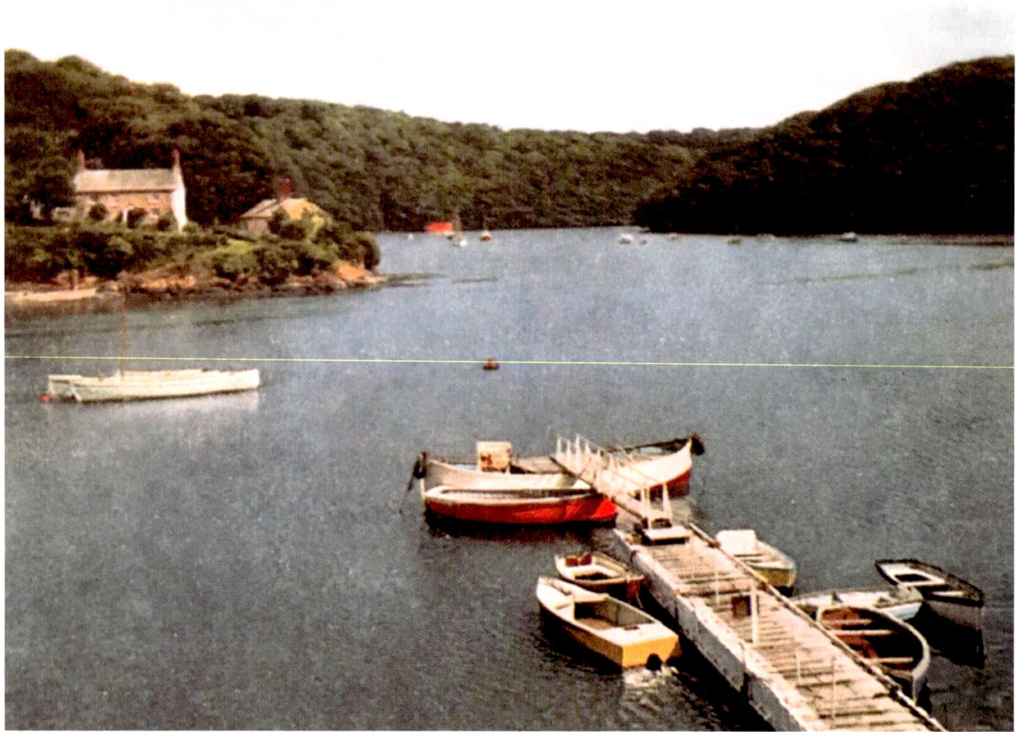

Boating at Malpas has always been a popular pastime for local people.

over to the boathouse at Tregothnan for picnics, an afternoon out or perhaps dancing or entertainment in the room over the boathouse. It was in 1804 that she became well known for saving Lord Falmouth's post from a thief – in fact, she caught the perpetrator.

Jenny Mopus, who died aged eighty-two, went down in local history for her reply when asked what was the biggest problem in her work on the ferry: 'Wemmin and Pigs'.

Trade in Tin

Throughout the 1500s, Truro was recovering from the hard times caused by an economic downturn. As things improved during the century, a merchant named Thomas Tregian amassed wealth by trading in tin. His earnings formed the basis of the Tregian family fortune, but unfortunately one of his deals led to a court case. Together with another man from Truro, he had entered into an agreement to sell tin to a London merchant in exchange for salt. At that time salt was extremely valuable, but before the deal could be done the price of salt plummeted, so they refused to take the salt and did not supply the tin, causing Tregian to be hauled before the courts. However, this episode did little to dampen his rise to riches.

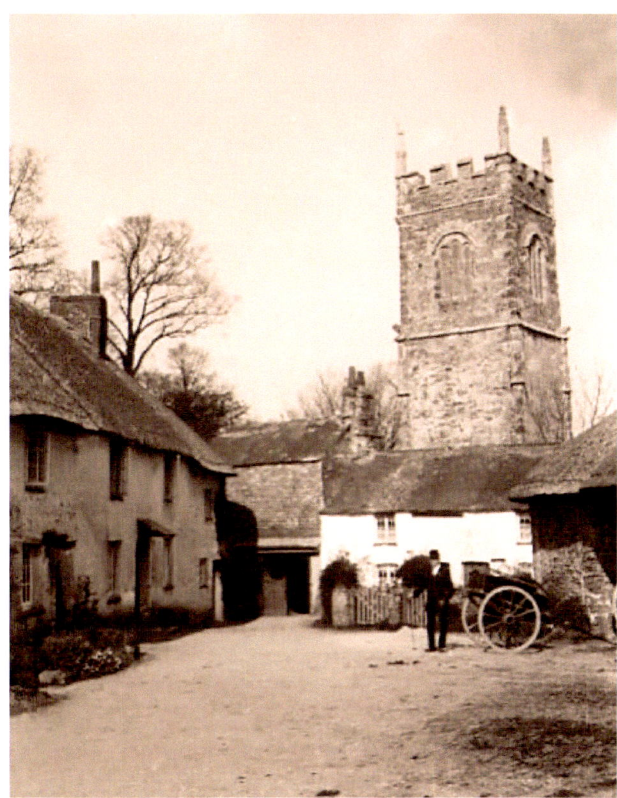

Right: Just around the corner from Lambessow is the village of St Clement, seen here in another era.

Below: This idyllic view of St Clement has changed little over the years.

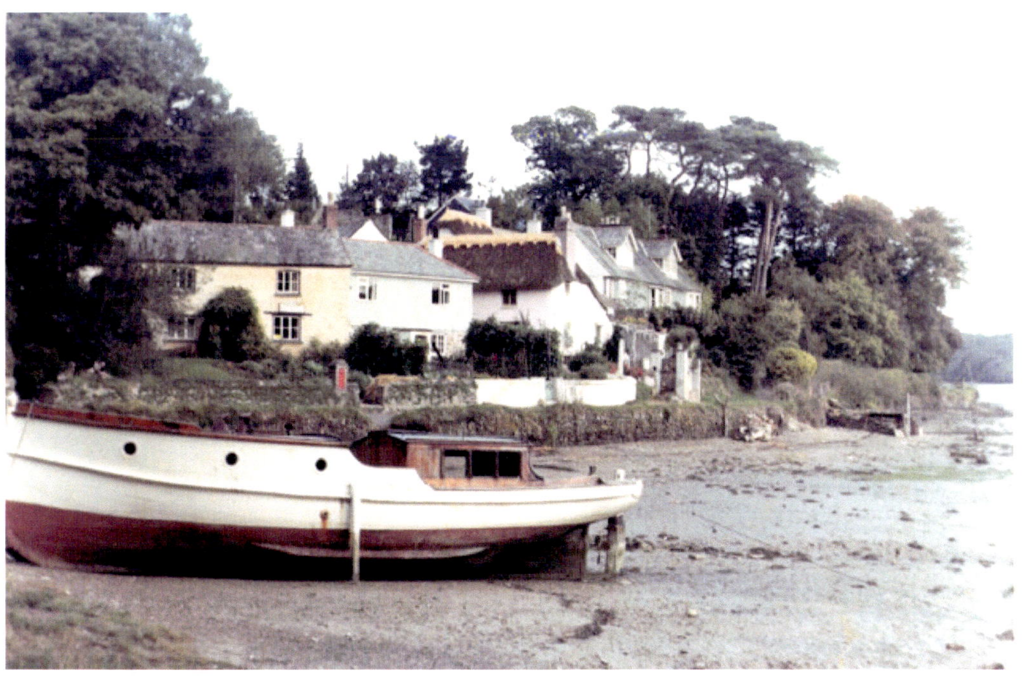

Helping the Poor

Many have experienced hardship throughout history, often due to unemployment, financial downturns or a lack of food or fuel. Mr H. L. Douch, in his *Book of Truro*, reminds us that in the eighteenth century the normal practice was to buy barley or flour at the going rate for sale to the poor at a lower price.

At one point, a meeting of the inhabitants of Truro and district was arranged to draw up a plan 'for the relief of the poor'. This consisted mostly of bedding and clothing; for food or fuel it was thought to be better to put the needy to work. In the meantime, new roads were required and many existing lanes and footpaths had become almost impassable through long neglect, so working on such improvements was delegated to the men among the hungry and needy.

The Truro–Malpas road is thought to have been carved out with this form of labour at the beginning of the nineteenth century. Colonel Boscawen promised the labourers a leg of mutton and 4 gallons of ale if they could cut through the intervening rock and finish the turning at Sunny Corner before a certain Saturday night, which the hungry men did. Many roads were cleared or made by such job creation schemes; that was a normal practice during this period. In 1909, the wall fronting Coronation Terrace was built by similar labour.

Various charities were set up to help the poor, especially for fuel, which was rarely affordable. John Cooper Furniss, who had a biscuit and sweet

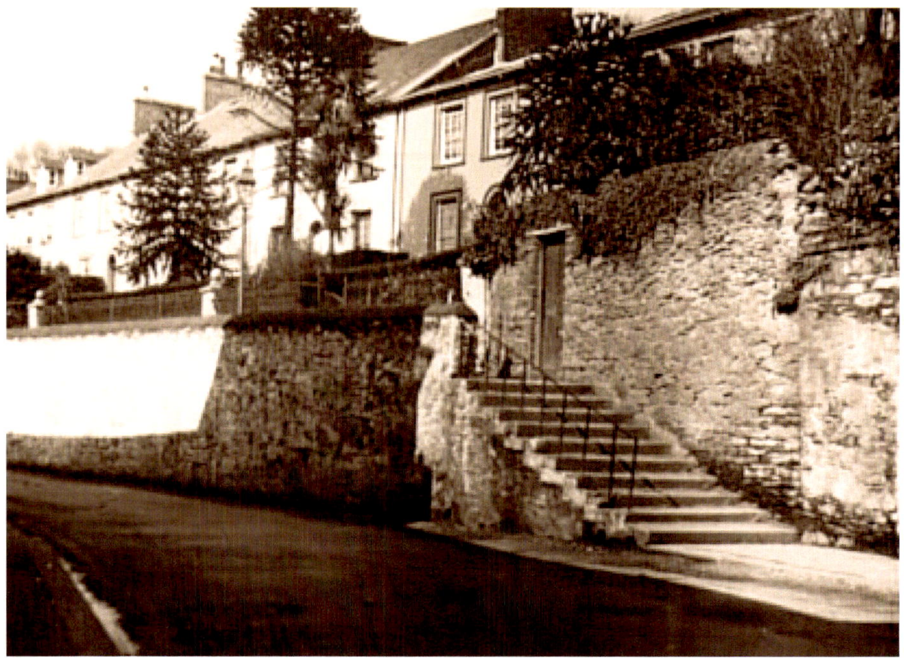

The steps at the end of The Parade were the starting point for the new road to Malpas.

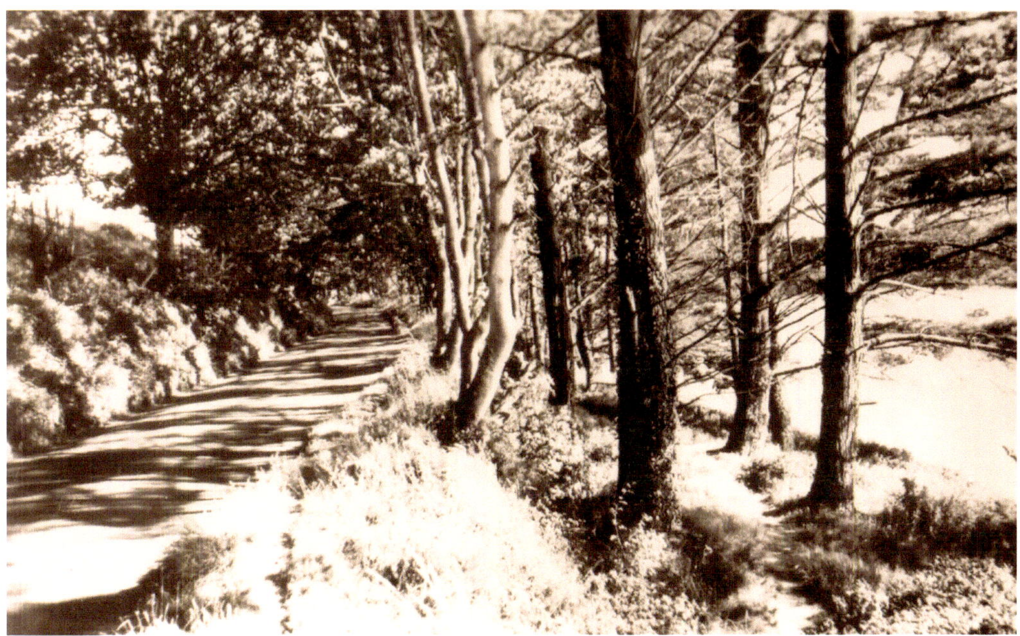

Sunny Corner was the finishing point of the road carved out by the hungry labourers.

factory, was a significant (and notably fair) employer in Truro and was well known as a philanthropist. In 1888 he set up the Furniss Coal Charity, which to this day provides free coal for residents of Truro who need it each November, even though Furniss' factory moved to Redruth in the 1980s. The Furniss Charity is still controlled by Truro City Council, but fewer people have coal fires, and is investigating the possibility of providing support for other forms of energy.

Hungry Tinners

Throughout the eighteenth century, the price of tin and copper was often depressed while corn was dear. Many tinners and their families were starving, and there was suspicion that farmers and millers were hoarding corn, driving up prices and causing greater hardship for the tinners. Angry mobs of tinners occasionally arrived in town, confronting the borough magistrates with their demands to be able to buy corn for their families.

In 1767, a similar mob arrived in Truro searching for corn. When they couldn't get any in the town, they went to Lambessow Farm in St Clement, a few miles away, and scoured the farm searching for sustenance. They finally seized and paid for the corn, but in the meantime one of the tinners stole a couple of silver spoons which were soon missed.

The ringleaders of the mob had no intentions to ransack the place, merely to buy the corn they had seized. Those in the mob were ordered to strip so that

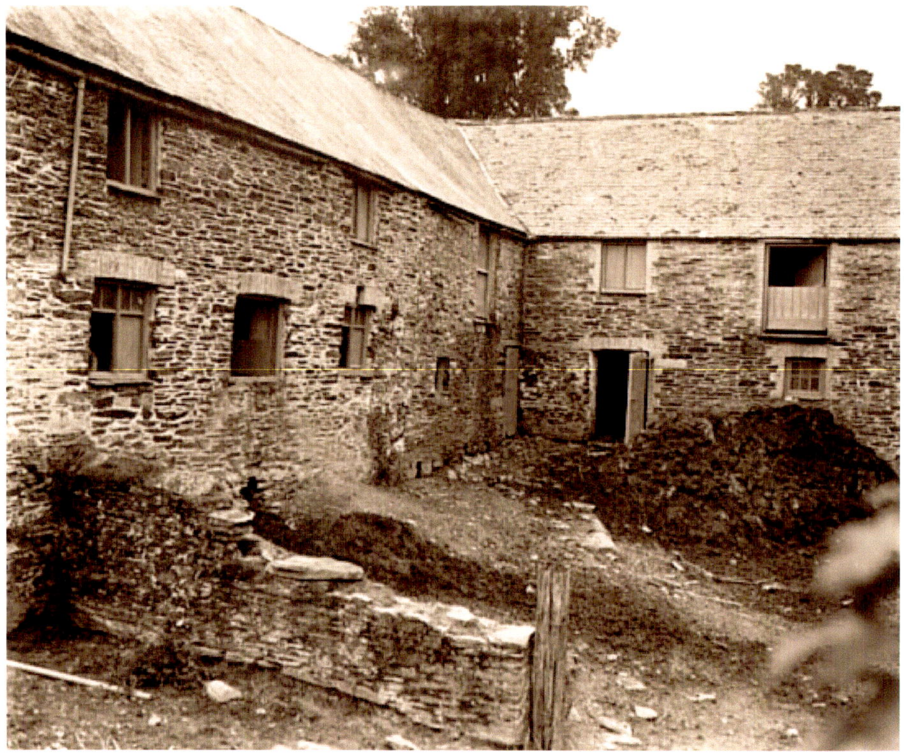

Steeped in history, Lambessow is believed to be the site of the former duchy prison. Seen here is a cowshed on the land before the house was renovated.

they might be searched. When one person refused, it was soon discovered who had filched the silver spoons. The thief was duly punished by being publicly stripped, tied to a post and subjected to 200 lashes, almost killing him. Such was the punishment in those times.

Egg Throwing

On 14 February 1988, a game that was to become a tradition arrived in Malpas. It was the Valentine's Day Smash, although from 1990 it became a feature of Easter Sunday.

Originally, a crowd would gather outside the Heron Inn and prepare to compete in an egg-throwing contest. The organisers bought the eggs, which had been rejected as too small to sell at the shop, then a team of two players paid £1 for two eggs. The throwing contest soon evolved into the Egg Smash. Competitors could buy a tray of eggs, knowing that one mystery egg had been adulterated with coloured dye that would become evident when it was smashed. The eggs were thrown at a board, and the thrower of the coloured egg would win a chocolate egg, with prize in question being anything from a Creme Egg to a more spectacular one depending on the year.

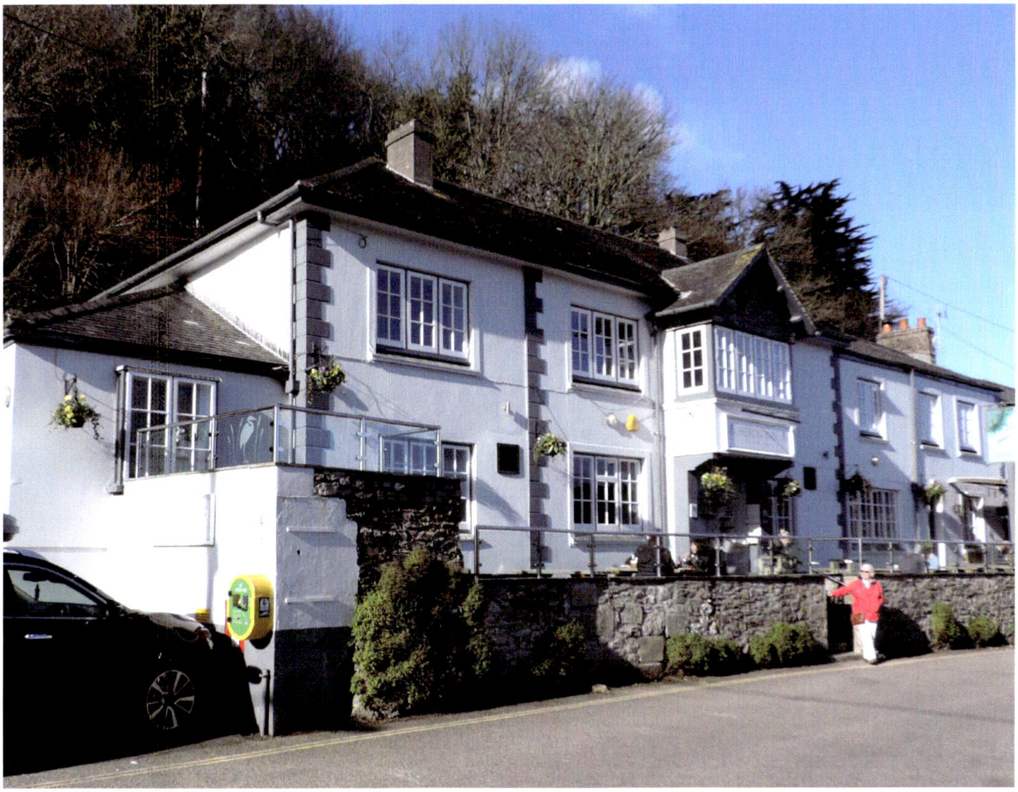

The Heron Inn, a popular restaurant and also the meeting place for the Egg Smash.

Still a popular
event today,
this photo
shows the
Malpas
Regatta in full
swing in 1909.

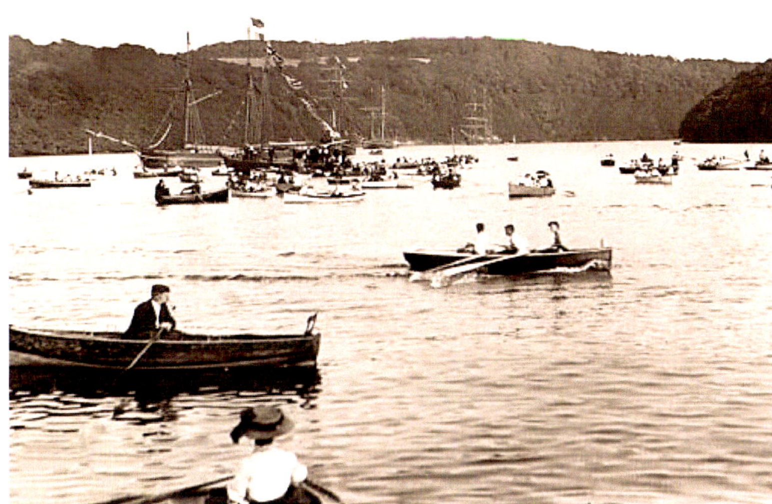

Russian Egglette was a little more dangerous: the team could buy a tray of eggs with an unknown one being hard boiled. To discover whether they were handling the raw egg or the cooked one, the two competitors smashed the eggs on each other's heads. The person who found the hard-boiled egg went through to the next part of the competition – possibly with a headache!

The Chicken Run, meanwhile, involved throwing eggs at a volunteer who would dash past the front of the Heron hoping to avoid being hit. Funds raised would go to the Regatta and prizes were always chocolate eggs. This continued beyond 2010, always being enjoyed with enthusiasm.

Hedgehog Roundabout

On the approach into Truro, visitors might well be surprised and amused when they arrive at the Trafalgar Roundabout to be greeted by four giant model hedgehogs strategically placed on the grassy traffic island in this busy thoroughfare. The spiky family, who appeared on the roundabout in 2019, are sponsored by a group from nearby Truro School known as the HOGS, which stands for Hedgehog Organisational Group Squad.

During the last five years the hedgehogs, costing £8,000, have brought great value and interest to the town and have even featured in national newspapers.

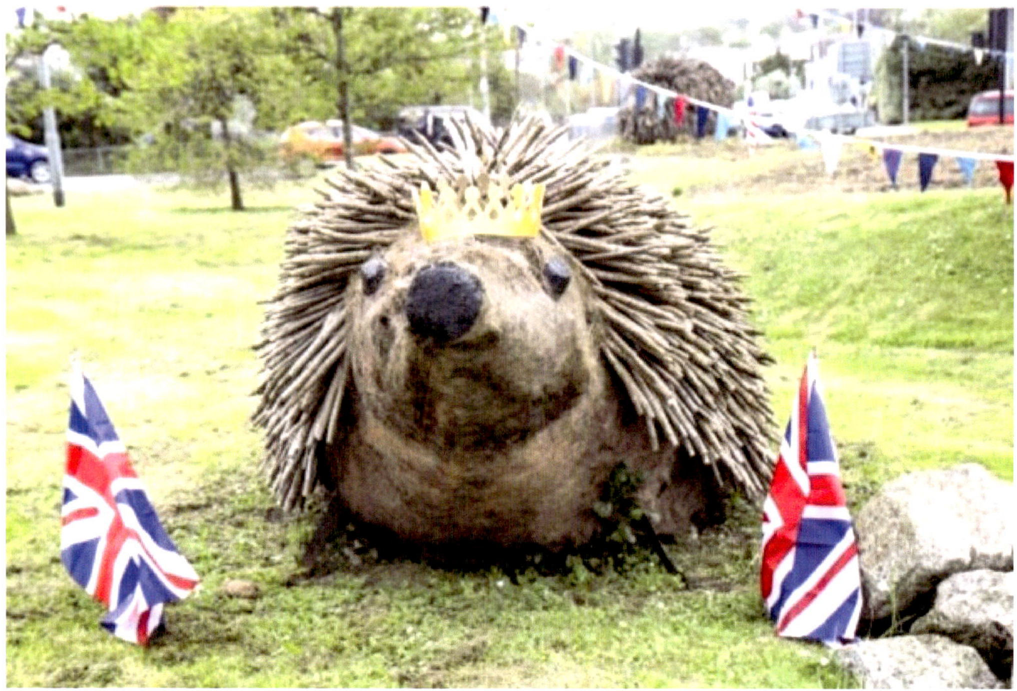

Truro's Hedgehog Roundabout has gained media fame. Denzil, one of the smaller hogs, has travelled to flower shows and also appeared on television as an entry for Britain in Bloom.

The hedgehogs celebrated the coronation of King Charles III with crowns, Union Jack flags and bunting.

Trafalgar Roundabout, now renamed locally as Hedgehog Roundabout, was awarded Roundabout of the Year in 2019 by the Roundabout Appreciation Society and also featured in the society's 2020 calendar.

The giant hedgehogs were designed by Padstow's Emma Scott and have been given the individual names Cecil, Patrica, Denzil and Kizzy.

Sadly, the hogs are now in need of repair because nesting birds have stripped the coco fibres from their faces. One at a time, the quirky foursome are being taken from their home at the roundabout for repairs using material from Devichoys Wood near Truro.

At Christmas, when the roundabout is decorated with lights and a special Christmas feature, it is time for the wooden hedgehogs to go into 'hibernation'. They are covered with old branches and sticks to protect them, and this act also raises awareness that 'real' hedgehogs are sadly in decline and need our help. It is suggested that during this time we should leave piles of leaves in our gardens so that the hedgehogs can use them to hibernate.

One of the smaller hedgehogs, Denzil, had a particularly busy year in 2024 as he attended the Chelsea Flower Show in May and the Royal Cornwall Show the following month. No doubt these spiky but beloved locals will bring fun and smiles to many more.

On the Home Front

Events

Truro's gasworks was among the first in the country, and by 1820 much of the town was lit by gas. Another use was found for the gas in 1832, however, when Mr Sambell's timber yard was home to a balloon for two days. It took that long to fill it with gas, and then a spectacular event took place to delight the people of Truro. A gentleman called Mr Graham was to ascend in the balloon; it apparently could rise as high as 4 miles, but fortunately it did not travel so far and in fact descended at Polwhele.

In 1856, the people of Truro wanted to celebrate not only Queen Victoria's birthday but also the end of the Crimean War. It was decided that a parade through the town showcasing some of the trades would be appropriate. Thomas

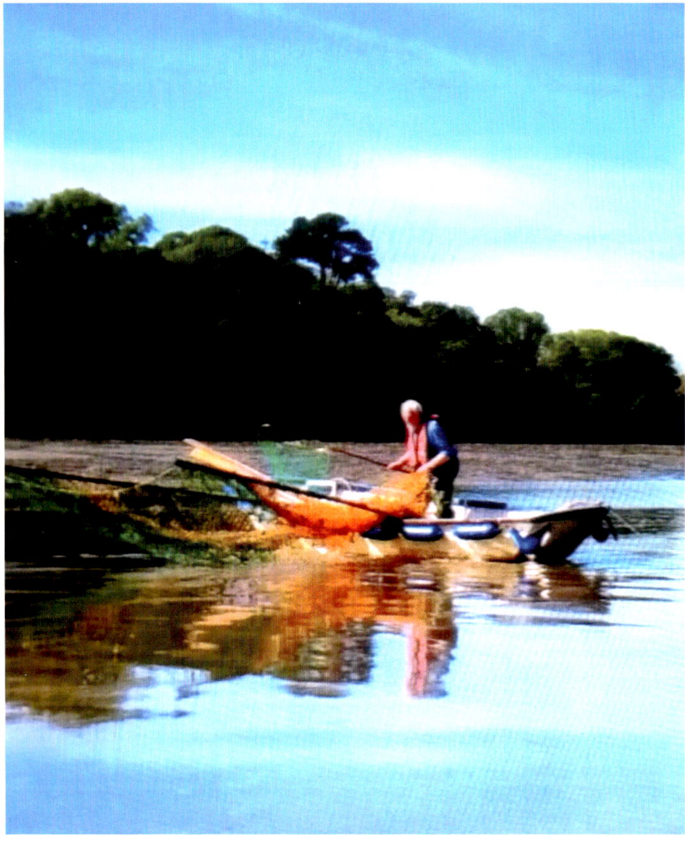

Jimmy Williams is seen here fishing for flat fish on an ebb tide on the Tresillian River.

Learwood made a chair that was presented to the mayor and later in his career invented a 'self-acting artificial leg'. This was the beginning of his most famous trade, so his business became the 'West of England Artificial Limb Manufacturer'.

In the past, not only did people live their lives in a different way but they earned their living differently. One example was Ann Hore, who was a lady blacksmith. After the death of her father, George Allen, she took over his Truro business and carried on trading.

Another occupation no longer seen is that of the lamplighter. A lady who lived in Boscawen Row in the early 1950s – although she was very young at the time – clearly remembers Fred Tippet lighting the gas lamp halfway down the street. She recalls that its glow did not reach where she lived, however, so not everywhere was supplied with gas lighting.

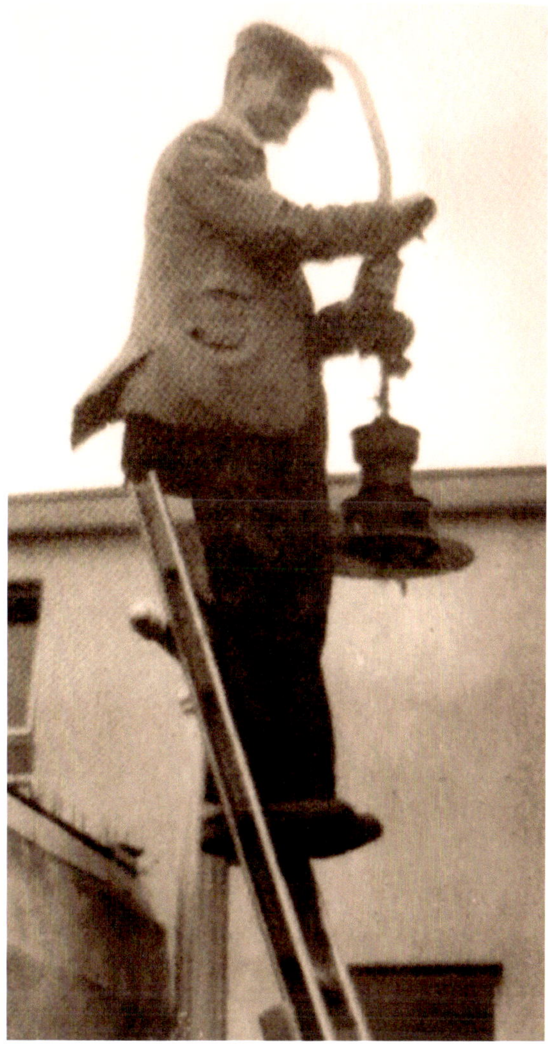

Fred Tippet no longer had to light the gas lamps as Fred Lance, seen here, had taken down the last of Truro's gas lamps in The Leats.

Dynamite

Cligga Head at Perranporth was the location chosen by the British and Colonial Explosion Company for their explosives factory to assist the mining industry. In 1892 it was bought by Alfred Nobel's company, and so dangerous was their dynamite that the premises were surrounded with an earth bank. The women employees took care to wear clothes and shoes that were safe in that environment and unlikely to cause a spark that could create a massive explosion. The dynamite was shipped across the world from Dynamite Quay in Truro, but any such transport first necessitated a journey through the town. Traction engines hauled loaded wagons through Boscawen Street, much to the dismay of the townsfolk. On one occasion a couple of boxes slipped from the wagon in Boscawen Street, but thankfully there was no explosion. People must have heaved a sigh of relief when the factory shut in 1905; although it briefly resumed work in 1915 as part of the war effort, it soon closed for good.

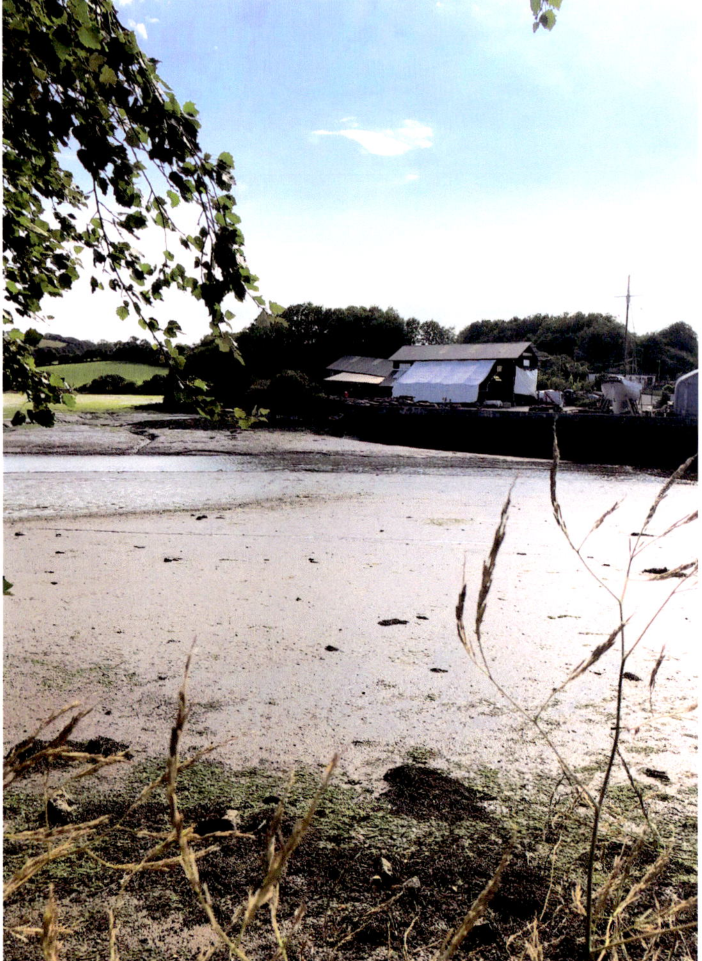

One of the quays situated along the Truro River. Lighterage Quay at Newham has reverted to its original name but was once known as Dynamite Quay.

Gas Explosion

In October 1927, an immense sound likened to a deafening gunshot followed by a booming noise left the people of Truro reeling. It soon became obvious that the number one gas holder at the Lemon Quay gasworks had exploded and caught fire. A report in the *West Briton* at the time stated that it had collapsed 'like a crushed biscuit tin'. Fortunately, it only took a few minutes for the fire brigade to attend and before long the blaze was extinguished and did not pose any danger to the other gas holders.

Two houses in Fairmantle Street were wrecked. Mrs George Gibbons lived with her children in one house and elderly Mrs Henry Gibbons in the other. Before the latter could be buried in debris, Mrs George Gibbons dashed from her home to

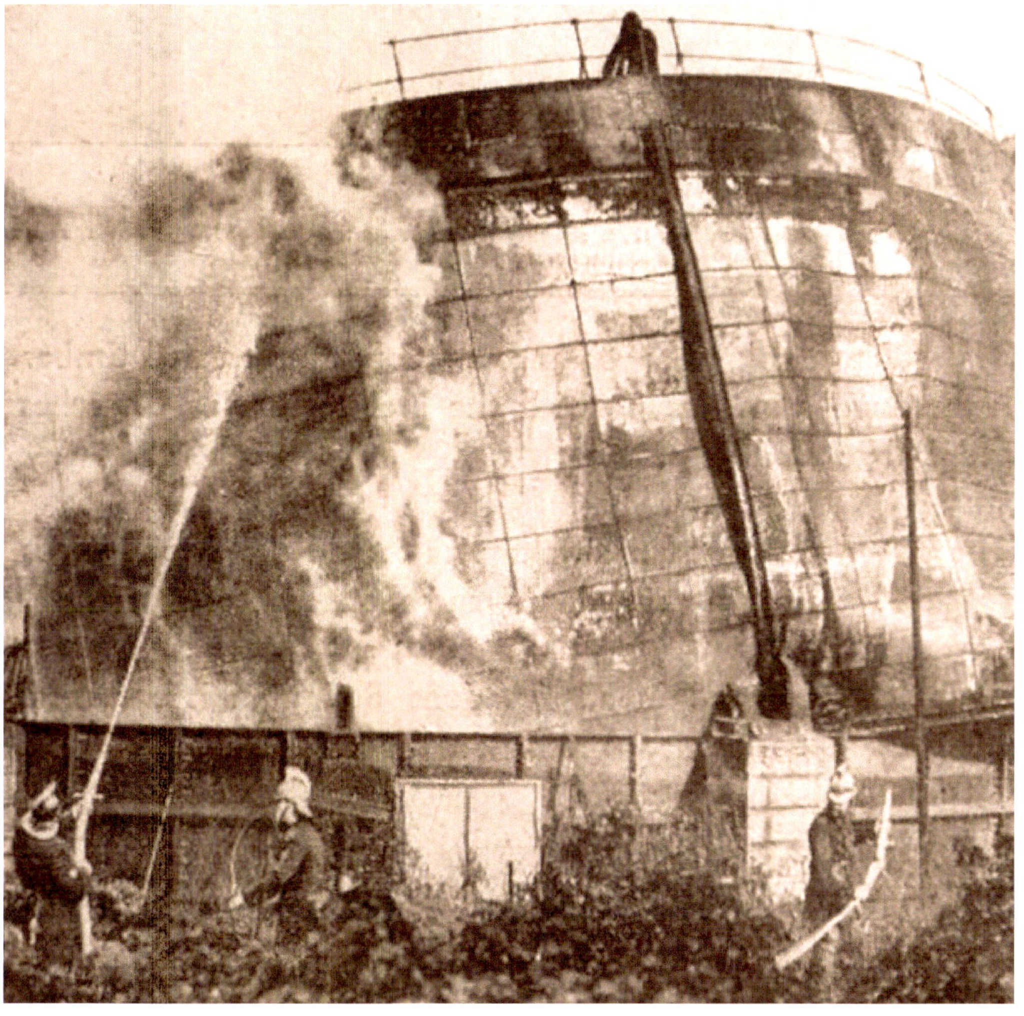

A photo in the *West Briton* in October 1927 shows firemen using their hoses on the conflagration caused by an explosion at the gasworks.

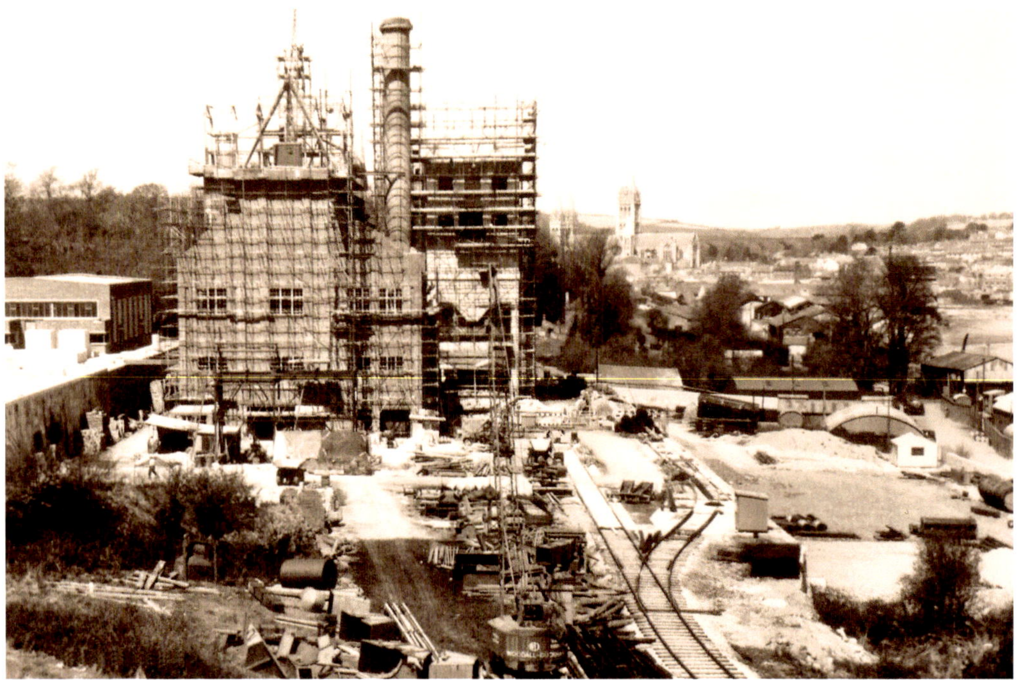

The new gasworks at Newham under construction in 1956.

seek help from neighbours and Mrs Henry Gibbons was led to safety. The two ladies suffered burns to their faces so they were taken to the Royal Cornwall Infirmary; like the children, their hair was also singed.

Mr Bray, an agent for the Brooke Bond tea company, had been standing on the pavement near the houses beside his car when the explosion occurred. Debris from the upper storeys fell on him and rescuers rushed to his aid. Although his car was crushed and he was knocked to the ground, the hood of the car had saved him. He was discovered up to his neck in debris, but was calm and still smoking his cigarette! Mr Bray was also taken to the Royal Cornwall Infirmary to be checked over. Mr Webb, a gas employee who lived across the road in a house called Ryderville, had his front windows broken; the power of the explosion spread the glass throughout the house.

Quick thinking teachers at the school on Fairmantle Street, meanwhile, did not bother wrapping the children in their coats and hats but quickly led the frightened and crying children away to safety.

About twenty-five years previously, gas holder number one had been blown over in a gale and a report suggested that it would cost as much to repair as to replace it. The gasworks was built sometime before 1902 and burned coal that arrived by river. In 1955, a new and bigger gasworks opened at Newham and was supplied by rail, but because of falling demand the Newham gasworks closed in 1969.

Hospital

Just as Truro had a community of Blackfriars (Dominican monks) living and working in the town, Bodmin had a community of Greyfriars. In the thirteenth century they established a hospital known as St Lawrence de Ponteboy. This hospital treated lepers and had the right to hold two fairs a year – St Lawrence Fair and St Luke Fair – to bolster the income received from their landholdings.

By 1809, the hospital was not fulfilling its duty of looking after lepers as the disease had more or less died out in this country. After a case in the Court of Chancery, the land and the right to hold the fairs was sold. The Royal Cornwall Infirmary was the buyer, and the purchase came with the legal quirk of a duty to care for any lepers. Ninety-eight years later, in 1907, a West Indian man suffering from leprosy entered the country, but it was decided that instead of keeping him in the grounds of the infirmary an alternative would be found. He did not want to return to his home so until 1912 he lived in the grounds of the Liskeard Workhouse.

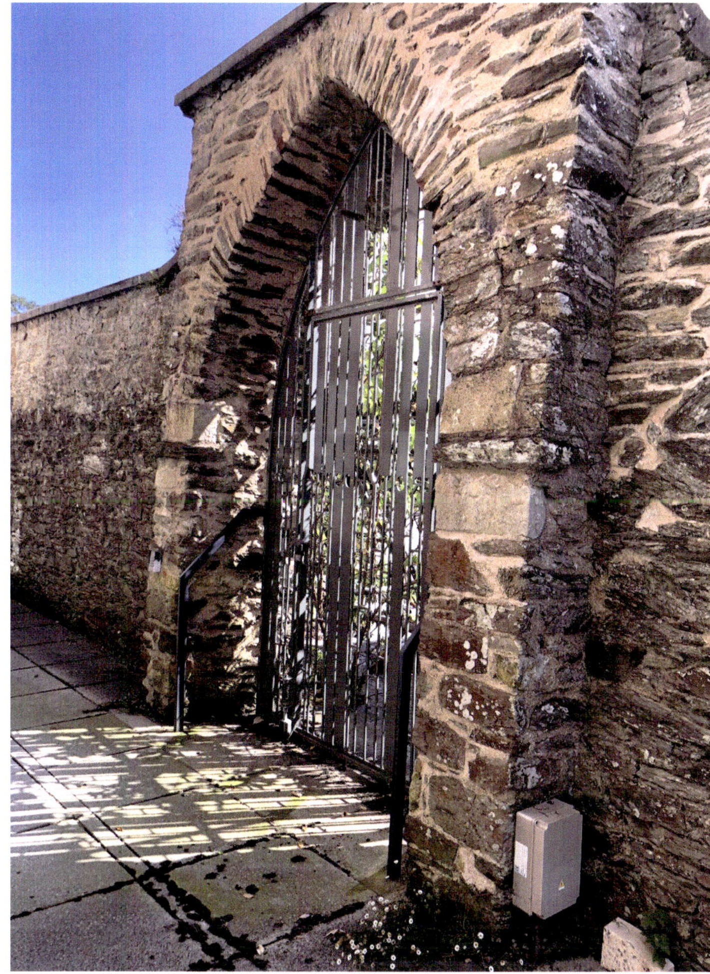

This view of the Leper's Arch was taken from the inside of the former hospital grounds. Scaffolding now supports the wall from the other side.

Truro is privileged to still have the gateway to the leper colony, known as the Leper's Arch. It is not in a very good state of repair, so it is not possible to walk through it. However, in the medieval era, when leprosy was rife in any port town, the afflicted souls would have passed through this very arch. It would lead roughly halfway up what is now Chapel Hill at Parkvedras Terrace, where the colony was sited. In more modern times, while the infirmary was still functioning and before Treliske Hospital opened, the arch led to the nurses' homes and gardens.

Charitable funding and voluntary helpers have played a very significant part throughout the history of the Royal Cornwall Infirmary. By the end of the nineteenth century the infirmary claimed to have a modest credit balance each year due to the wonderful support and voluntary effort offered by various organisations such as the Samaritan Fund, the Hospital Saturday Fund and the Hospital Sunday Fund, which regularly held concerts and garden fetes. There were also numerous donations for the medical staff, hospital equipment and the hospital's future progress. The first fete to be held at the Royal Cornwall Infirmary occurred in 1898 and was held in aid of the Samaritan Fund. This fund had been established the previous year to help poor patients who were unable to afford their medical appliances. Patients were required to pay for artificial limbs, which were the most expensive items, and also for splints and treatment of fractures. In later years fetes were held in various country houses with large gardens. Eventually, the hospital fete became an annual event in the grounds of the infirmary.

Among the many organisations helping the hospital was a group of volunteer ladies known as the Linen League. Founded in 1911 by Mrs Panting, the wife of a senior surgeon, it started with thirty members. By the time of the next year's meeting that number had risen to ninety-three. These ladies aimed at keeping the infirmary supplied with linen; however, more than just keeping the linen cupboard filled, with the help of the Cornwall Needlework Guild they carried the heavy burden of mending where necessary.

In May 1936, the *West Briton* reported on the twenty-seventh annual meeting of the Linen League, during which Miss Mabel Smith claimed the year had been one of their most satisfactory to date. She commented that in former years a large source of their income had been dances and concerts, but it was now necessary to knock on doors. The league now had a willing band of collectors happy to approach the public, often with pleasing results. After the First World War, women took an important role in a wide variety of hospital activities; in 1920 they made their first appearances on management committees.

The Royal Cornwall Infirmary was not always the healthiest place to be. In 1868, Dr Slyman Michell died of typhoid aged only fifty-one. Typhoid was again a problem in 1878, killing Mrs Marsh, the wife of the house surgeon, among others. The main drain had been installed in Infirmary Hill in 1853, but it seemed that nobody had connected it to the infirmary drains. At one point, sanitary conditions forced the closure of the hospital for four months.

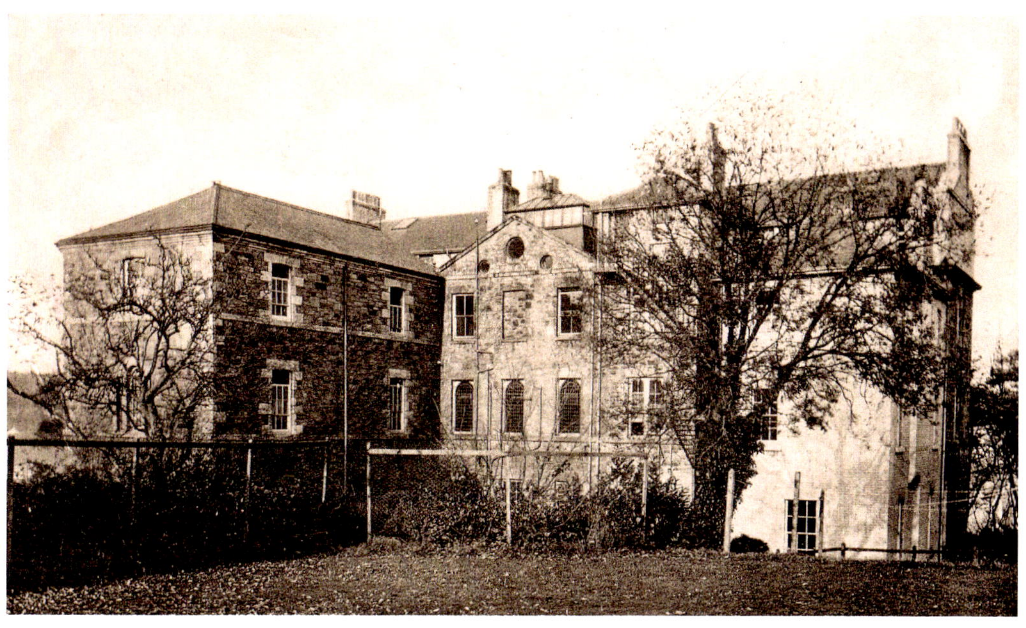

An unusual view of the back of the Royal Cornwall Infirmary.

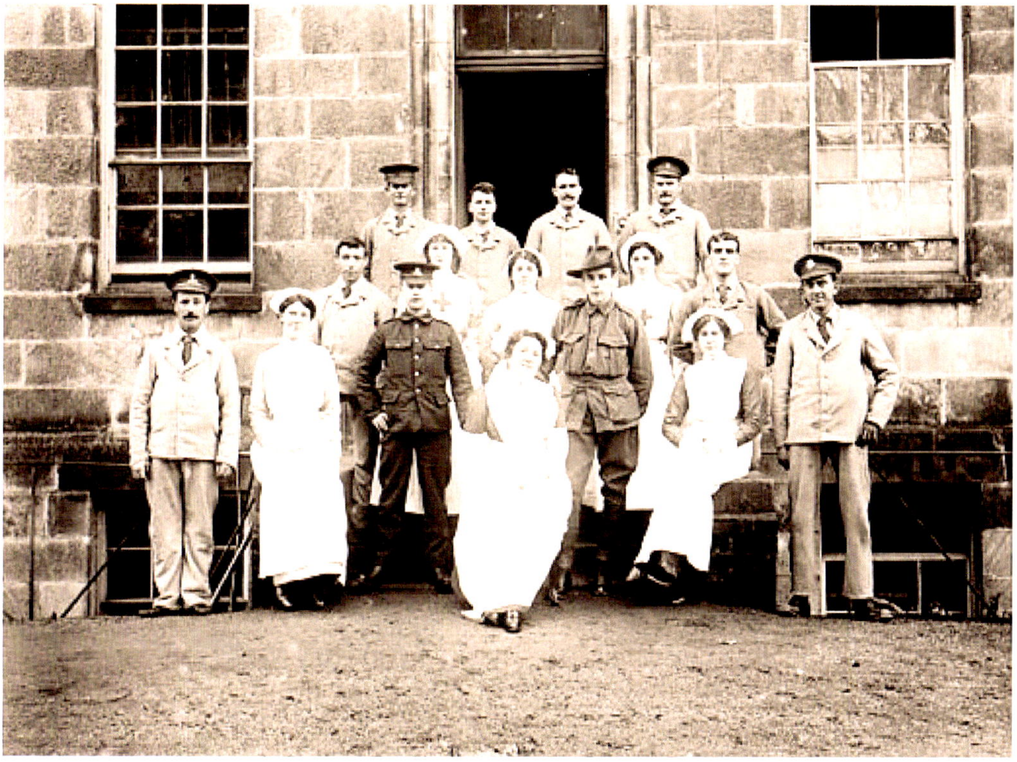

Hospital staff of the Royal Cornwall Infirmary pose with patients during the First World War.

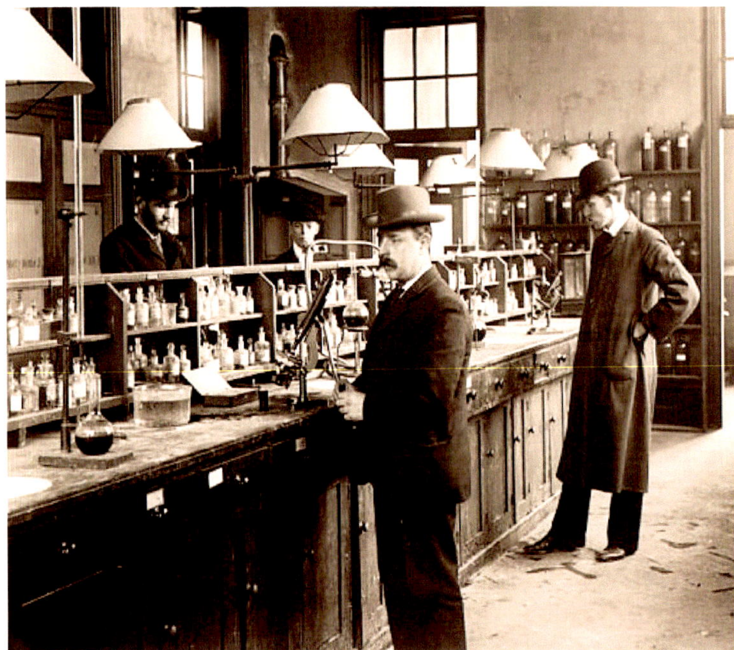

Left: This laboratory in Truro Technical School during the 1900s would not have looked out of place in the early hospital.

Below: Rarely to be found in Cornish kitchens today, this pair of Cornish ranges is an interesting feature still to be found in 18 Lemon Street.

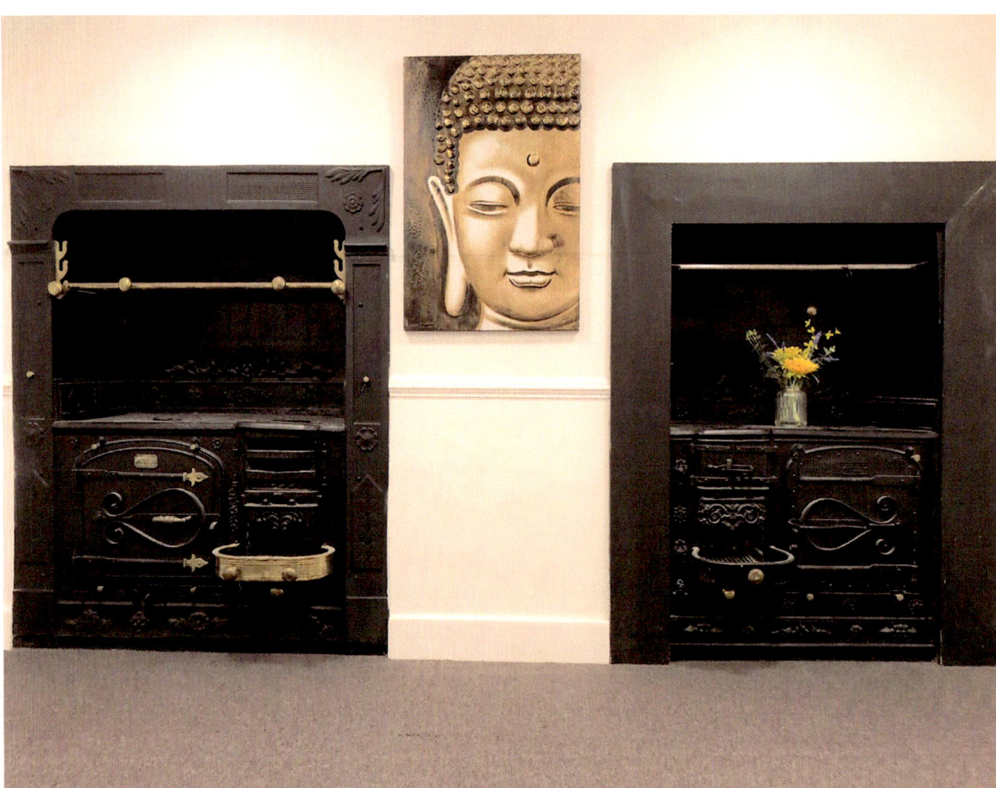

Diseases such as typhoid, smallpox, scarlet fever and diphtheria were rife in Truro and were attributed to drains, water pumps and the state of sanitation in the town. The rivers Allen and Kenwyn were polluted with household waste. In Douch's *Book of Truro* it is stated that 'pigs were everywhere in the town'. The town clerk was instructed to draw up a bylaw for 'the more effectual preventing persons from suffering their hogs or swine to run loose about this borough'. To give an idea of the scale, in 1874 a pork butcher was said to have slaughtered 716 pigs, and an estimated 42 tons of meat had been reared on refuse which would have polluted the rivers.

There are still many local people today who will remember 18 Lemon Street as the place to go for an appointment with the doctor. It was known as the Lower Surgery to distinguish it from the one a few doors up the road, which, unsurprisingly, was called Upper Surgery. The unusual thing was that it had been operating for more than two centuries. It was in 1806 that the first doctor opened his practice in No. 18, and it was only closed in 2010 when the practice relocated to Truro Health Park in the grounds of the old infirmary, which was ideally situated to accommodate updated facilities. The lower surgery is now Three Spires and the upper is Lander. The health park also provides other medical services and has ample parking.

Tanks

After the First World War, 265 towns had a surprise gift. According to reports at the time it was by no means certain that this gift was welcomed, but as a thank you for the efforts of the townsfolk in buying bonds and certificates to raise money, they were to be given a tank!

It was advertised that the tanks had seen active service and were returning from Flanders and France, but it transpired that many had been used for training purposes only.

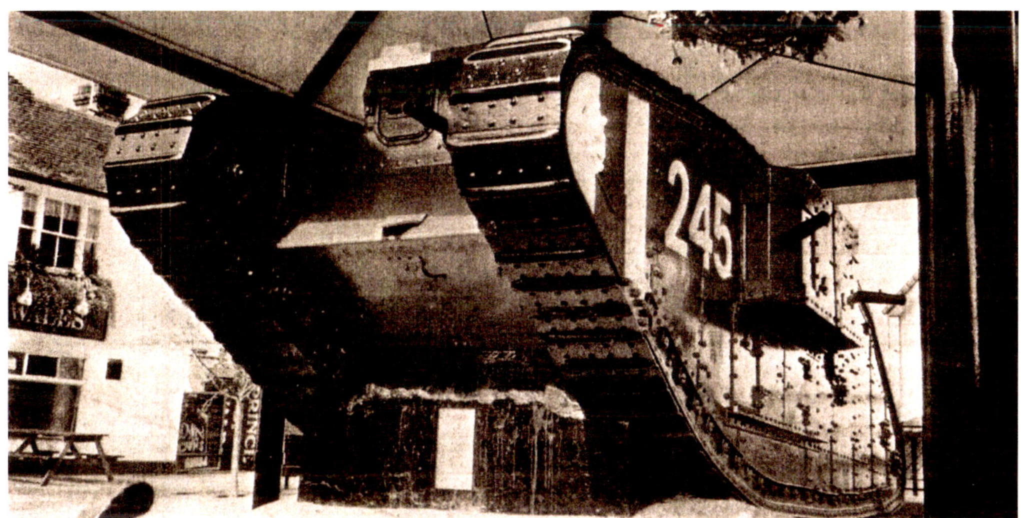

One of the First World War tanks that were gifted to many towns, including Truro.

It is believed that Truro's tank had a difficult time in our narrow streets and became wedged when turning from Kenwyn Street into Little Castle Street, but the people who would have seen it are no longer around to verify the tale. Indeed, it might not be true as many of the tanks gifted in this way arrived by rail and Truro's should have had an easy drive to its resting place in Victoria Gardens.

Most of the tanks around the country were scrapped during the Second World War, perhaps with some of the metal being used for the new war effort.

Cora Ball

On 15 October 1922, a large crowd gathered in Boscawen Street to witness the unveiling of the war memorial. Truro's mayor, N. B. Bullen, asked J. C. Williams, Lord Lieutenant of Cornwall, to unveil the memorial accompanied by the troops presenting arms and observations of the 'Last Post', the 'Reveille' and one minute's silence. The ceremony continued with prayers and hymns, then concluded with the national anthem and a march-past by schoolchildren. Members of the public were then at leisure to place any tributes on the memorial and study the names of the men of Truro who fell in the First World War.

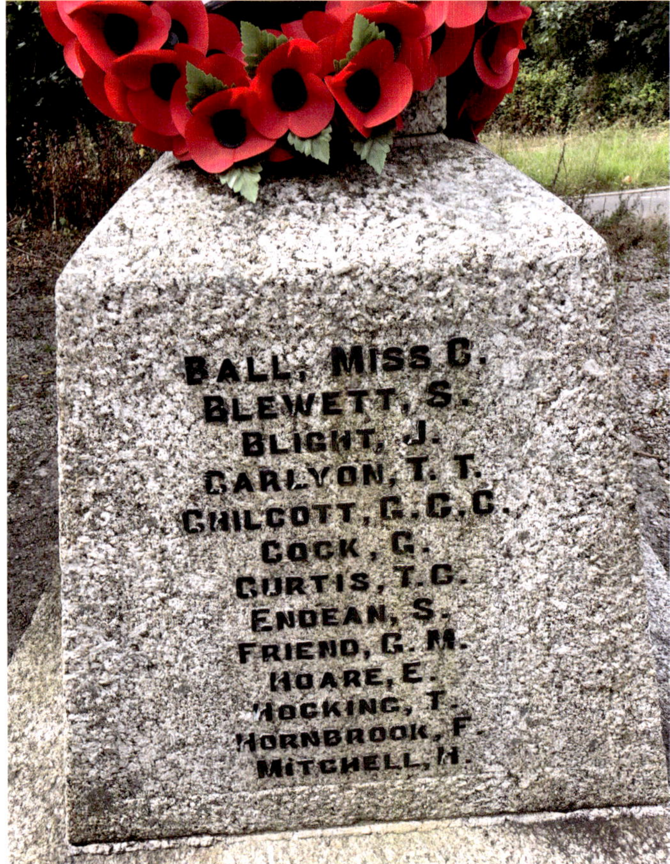

Cora Ball tops the list seen here on the Kenwyn War Memorial. Her name is also included on the Truro War Memorial in Boscawen Street.

At the end of the list of those lost were four words: 'And Miss Cora Ball'. Cora Cornish Ball, the only lady on the memorial, was born in 1896 and for a time lived in Kenwyn, which in those days was a village just outside Truro. She came from a large family but stayed at school until she was fourteen years old. In 1917 she joined the Queen Mary's Army Auxiliary Corps and served in France. She was promoted to the rank of forewoman, which was equivalent to a sergeant in the army, and was awarded the British War Medal and the Victory Medal. Tragically, she died aged only twenty-two on 24 November 1918, just a few days after the Armistice. Her war grave is in Les Baraques Military Cemetery at Sangatte.

Her name not only appears on the Truro War Memorial but also on the roadside memorial at Kenwyn. She was included in the Centenary celebrations in the Unremembered Project marking the women workers and multinational Labour Corps of the First World War.

Home Guard

Truro had several Home Guard detachments in the Second World War, and they were largely made up of First World War veterans.

The experiences of two men from the gasworks, Frankie and Arthur, were mentioned in the literature published to mark the Centenary. One early morning while they were on patrol at Lemon Quay, a man appeared out of the gloom on his way to work. Frankie leapt into action, levelling his rifle and demanding, 'Let's see your 'dent'ty card.'

It was produced and Frankie said, 'You look Arthur, you d'knaw I kint read.'

Arthur replied, 'Tis no good giving 'n to me Frankie, I 'an't got me glasses.'

Truro was in safe hands!

Bombing of Truro

It is well known that Truro was bombed during the Second World War, with the hospital taking a direct hit that caused much damage and loss of life. What is not so well known is that during that air raid there was structural damage to St Paul's Church. For ten years or more the church has been empty and up for sale, and it was only when plans began for developing the crypt as a social space that the surveyors discovered the extensive problems caused by the hit. A seven-figure sum was estimated to rectify the damage caused by the bombing.

Other damage during this air raid was sustained on the outskirts of Threemilestone on the main railway line between Truro and Penzance. An account of the bombing was written by Mr K. W. Hill, who was an eight-year-old evacuee at the time. The hit caused a fire on the railway embankment and everyone turned out to help extinguish the blaze so that the blackout curfew could be maintained. Much to the delight of the young boy, a horse-drawn fire engine attended, accompanied by seven firemen who worked the wooden side of the water pump.

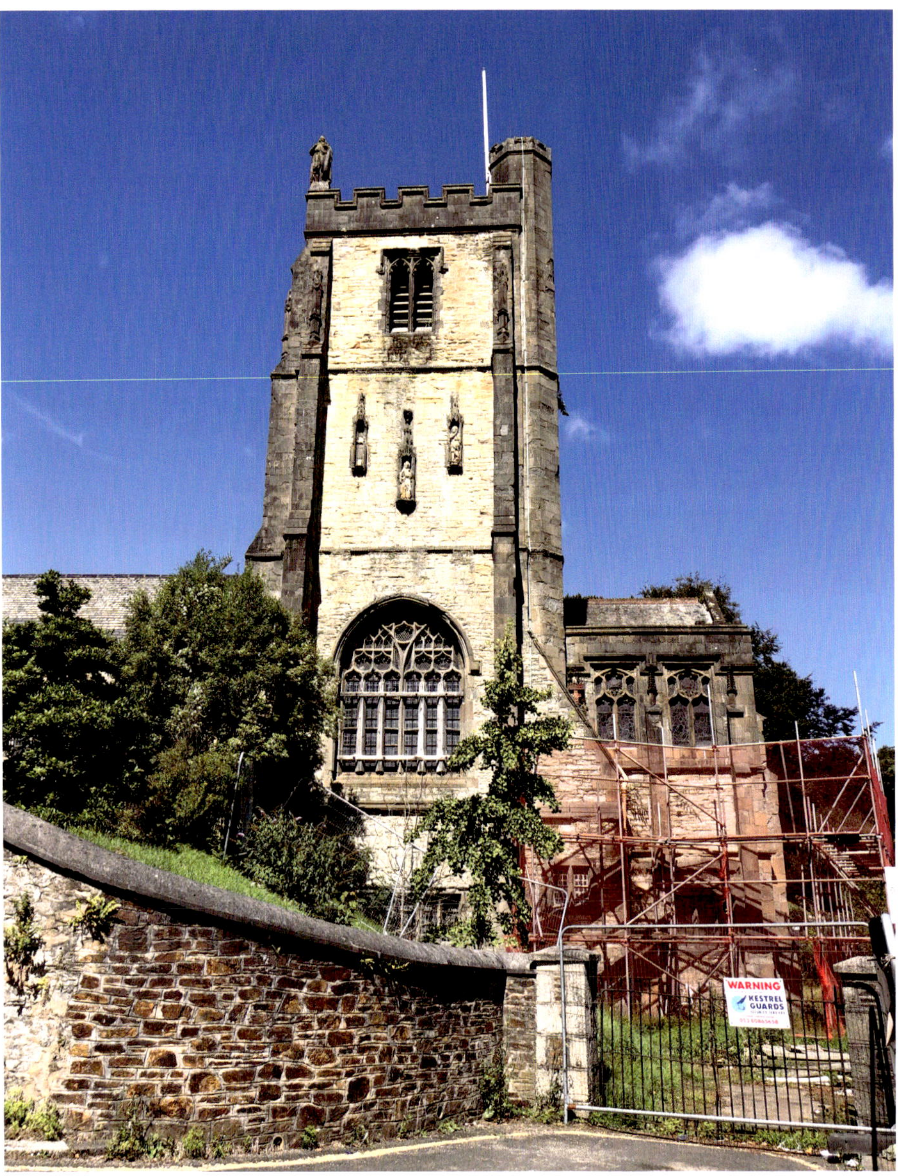

Now in a state of disrepair, St Paul's Church is no longer in use because of damage to the crypt during the Second World War bombing of Truro.

Bert Barberry was also a young boy in Truro during the war, and his father worked in a large garage. One day, a car belonging to Hitler's second-in-command, Herman Goering, was shown to the public. It was a thrilling experience for young Bert as he was placed in the driver's seat by his father. He was later taken to an air display where he saw the famous 'flying bedstead' aircraft. It certainly looked like a bedstead, and it took off vertically. This was in fact a prototype of the modern helicopter and the beginning of VTOL (vertical take-off and landing) craft. In 1949 he also witnessed a Bristol Brabazon fly over Truro. One of the largest aircraft ever made at that time, and designed to take 100 passengers, it was never put into service and there was only one made.

No doubt these boyhood memories will be retold to future generations.

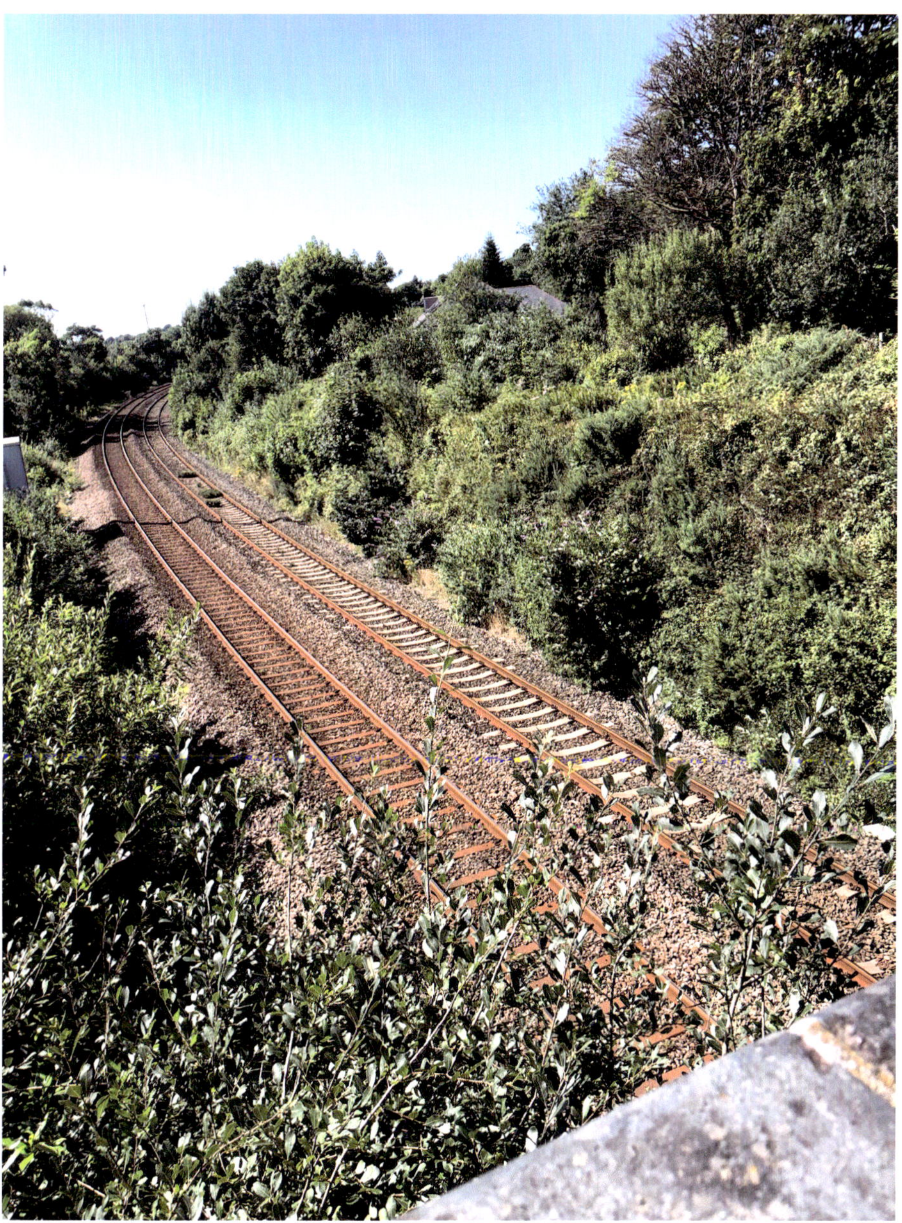

A photo taken from the railway bridge at Threemilestone shows the area of the embankment that was bombed and caught fire during the Second World War.

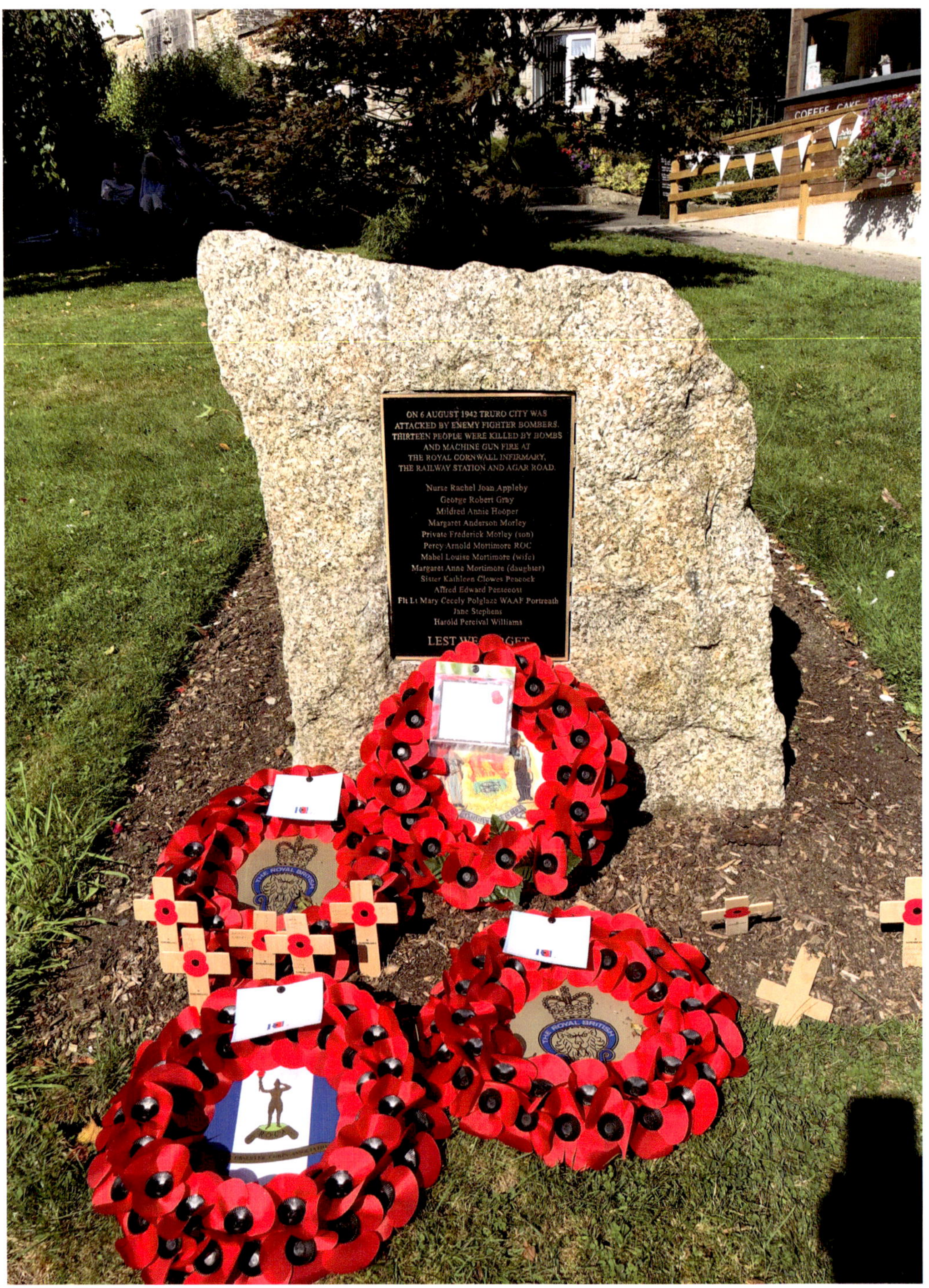

Victoria Gardens is home to a memorial plaque in memory of the thirteen people who were killed during the bombing of Truro on 6 August 1942.

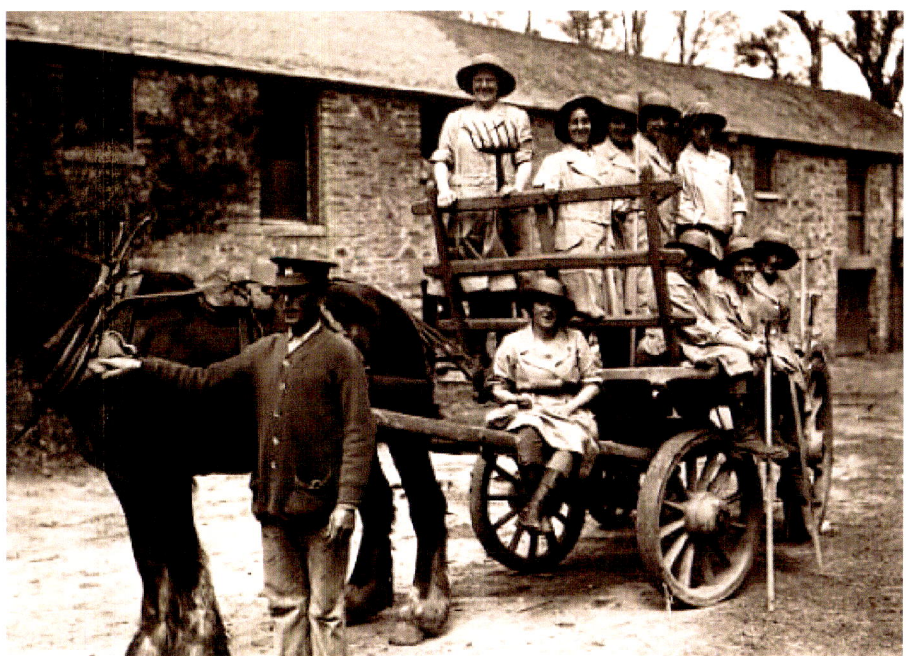

Tregavethan Farm near Threemilestone was a training centre for the Women's Land Army during the Second World War. Nine members are seen here on a horse-drawn wagon in their working clothes.

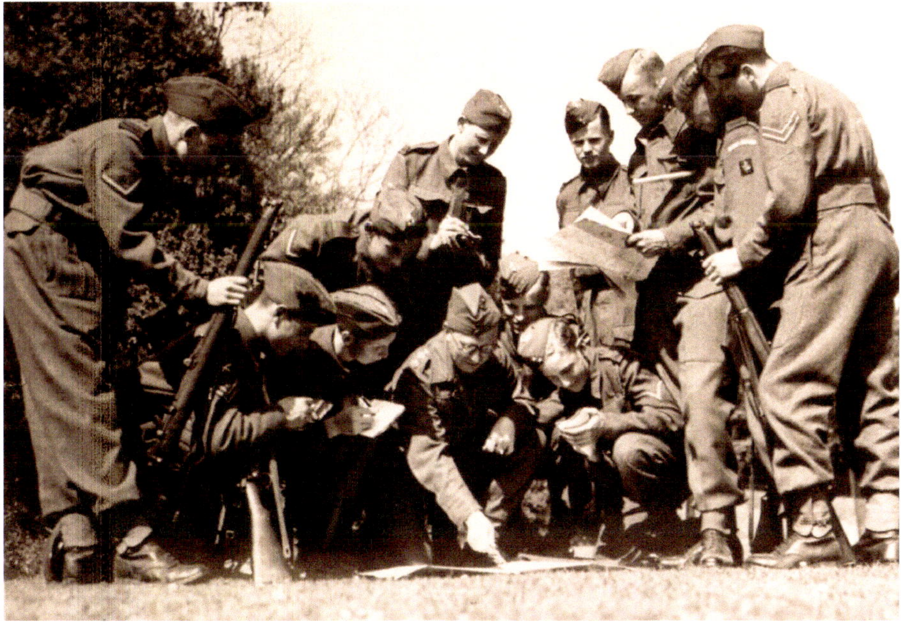

The Home Guard at Malpas in 1941 had special responsibility for protecting the petrol depot and the river.

Wheels, Wings and Other Things

Railway Arch

In the 1850s, the coming of the railway brought much interest and excitement to the people of Truro. It began to arrive piecemeal in 1852, when the line from Truro to Penzance, but trains to and from Devon were still a few years in the future.

Truronians seemed to have a liking for building celebratory arches, as we have seen in the earlier passage on the laying of the foundation stone of the cathedral. This time, the unlucky arch spanned Tregolls Road between the police station and the Union Hotel.

Unfortunately, no one had told the driver of the mail coach that the arch had been built and not only was it dark as the coach approached the town but the structure was not well lit. The coach made it through, but the beam across the top of the arch dislodged some luggage stored on the roof and knocked a passenger into the road, at which point he was run over. He was taken to the Union Hotel,

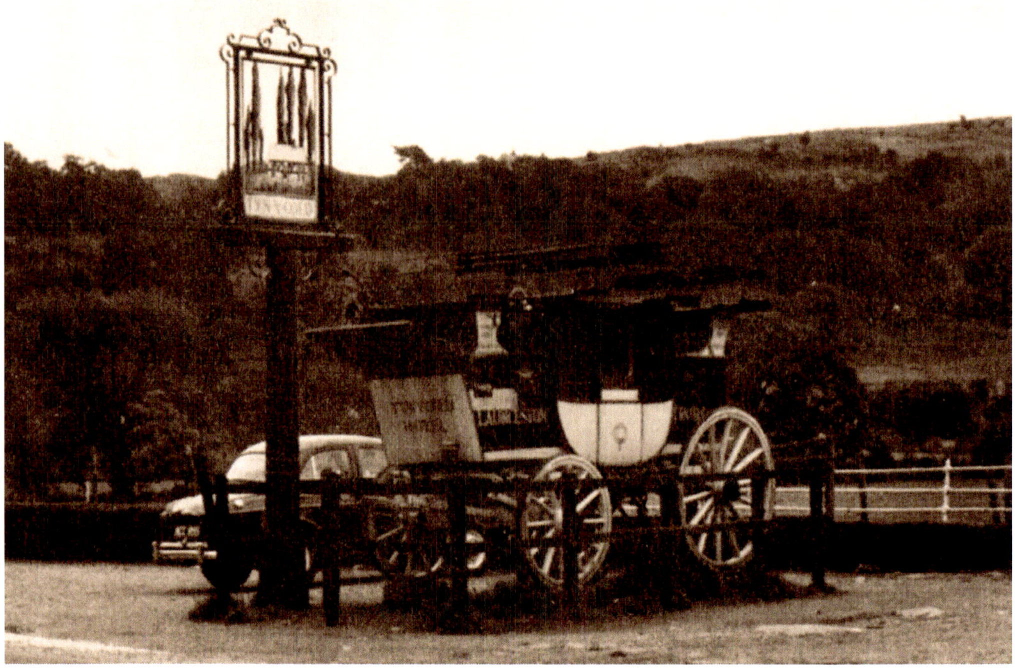

This coach would have been the type used to convey passengers and mail. It had Truro and Launceston emblazoned on the side, so obviously had seen service throughout Cornwall.

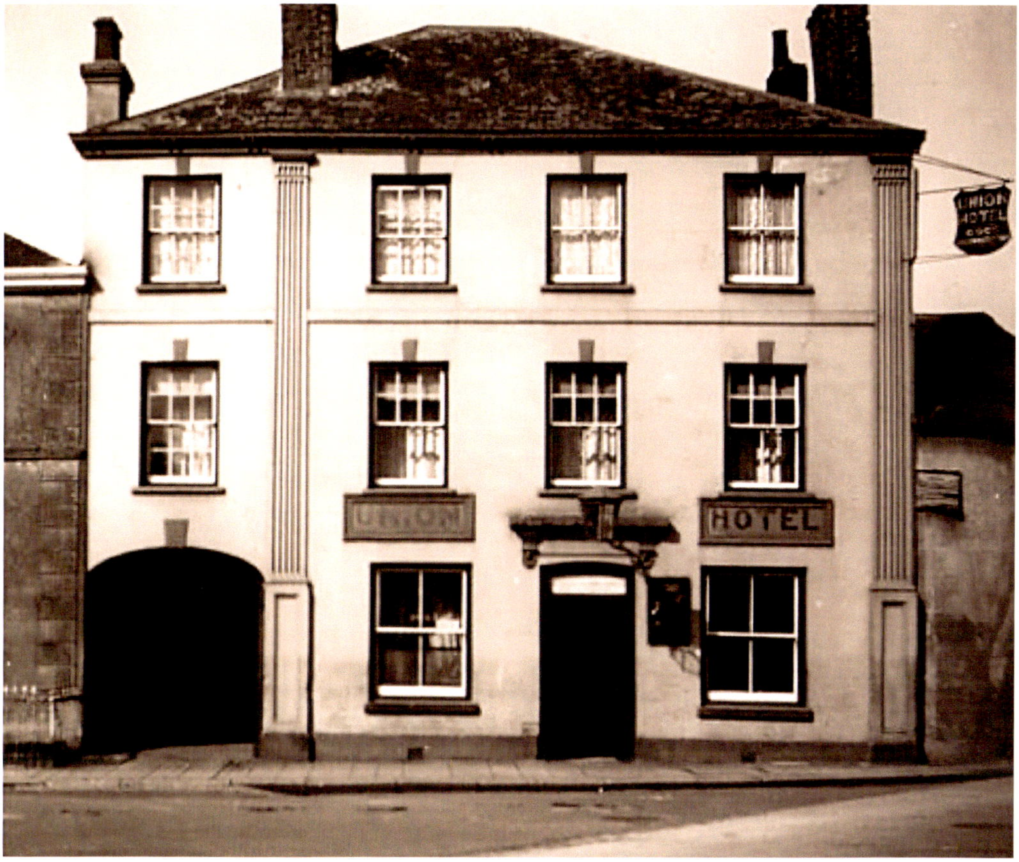

Above: The Union Hotel was opposite the police station, where the railway arch was sited.

Right: This delightful picture shows one of two horse-drawn carts loaded with the Kenwyn church bells on the way to Loughborough to be recast in 1905.

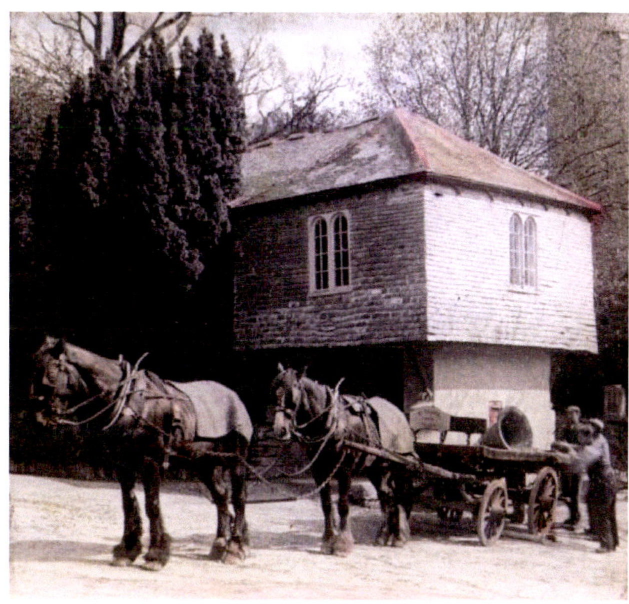

but he sadly died soon after. It could have been even worse; the guard, William Bilkey, was about to stand up to blow the post horn when he heard the crash.

In the verdict of accidental death delivered by the coroner, 'the improper construction of an arch' was mentioned. Before long the mail coach would no longer be in service, losing its role to the railway celebrated by the ill-fated arch.

City of Truro Locomotive

On Christmas Eve 1801, a steam locomotive prototype, the brainchild of Richard Trevithick, climbed up Camborne Hill. By 1804 his locomotive was at the Penydarren Ironworks in Glamorganshire pulling wagons loaded with iron ore and transporting men. A few years later, on the spot where Euston station

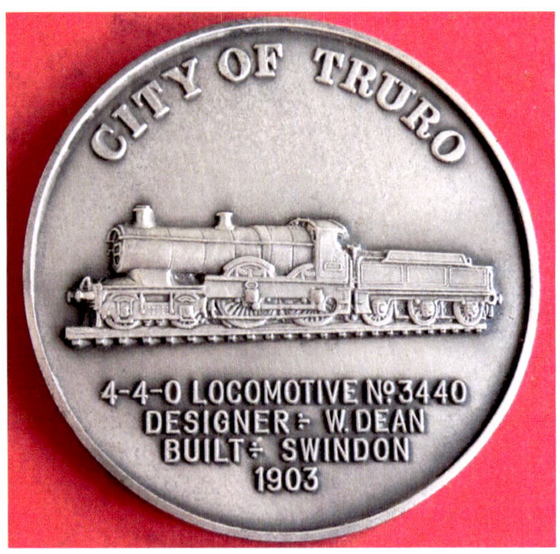

Left: A commemorative medal of this special locomotive.

Below: Truronians are proud of the famous *City of Truro* locomotive, and there is always an enthusiastic welcome whenever it visits the local area.

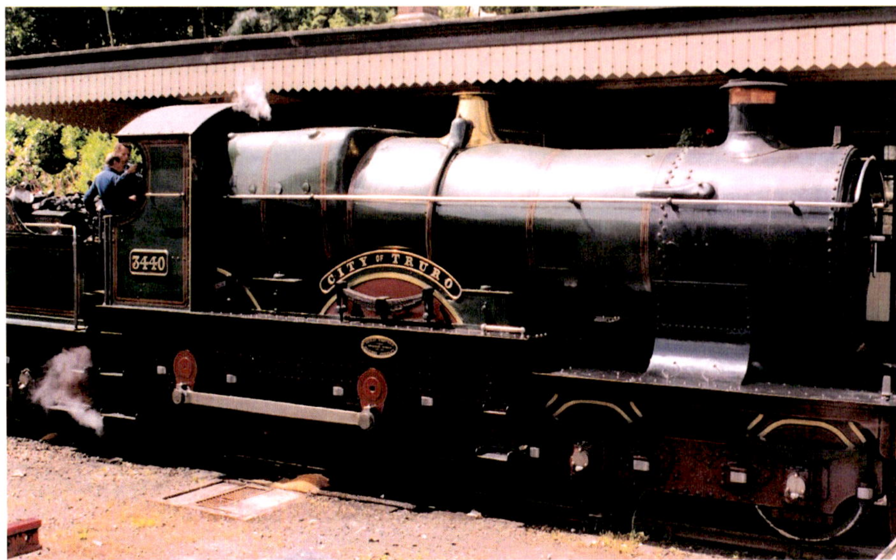

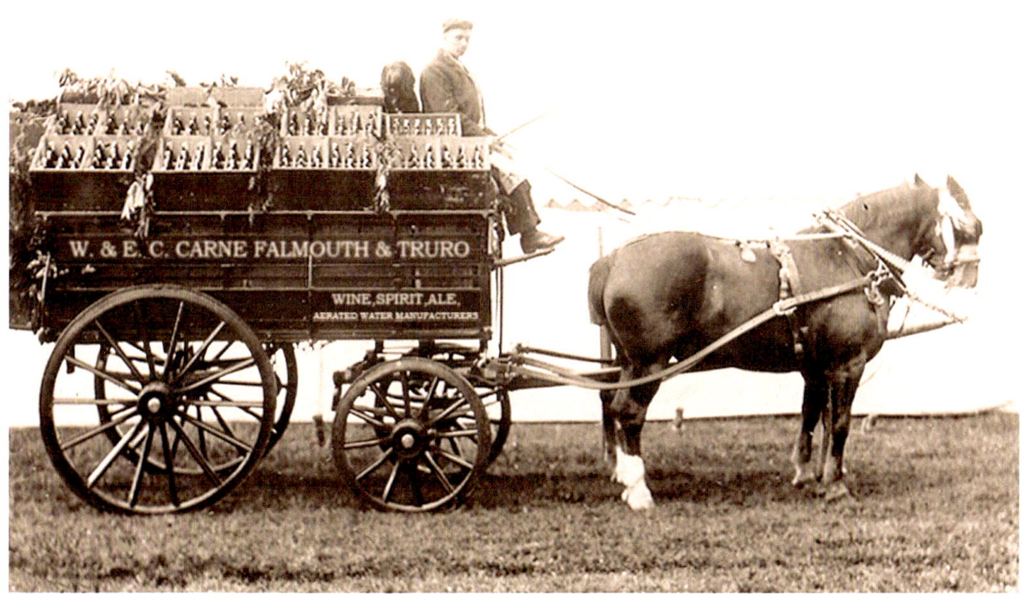

Above: The delivery cart is loaded not only with wines and spirits but aerated water from the malt brewery in Carnes Ope.

Right: Cyclists at High Cross in 1925, proving that the bicycle was a popular mode of transport back then.

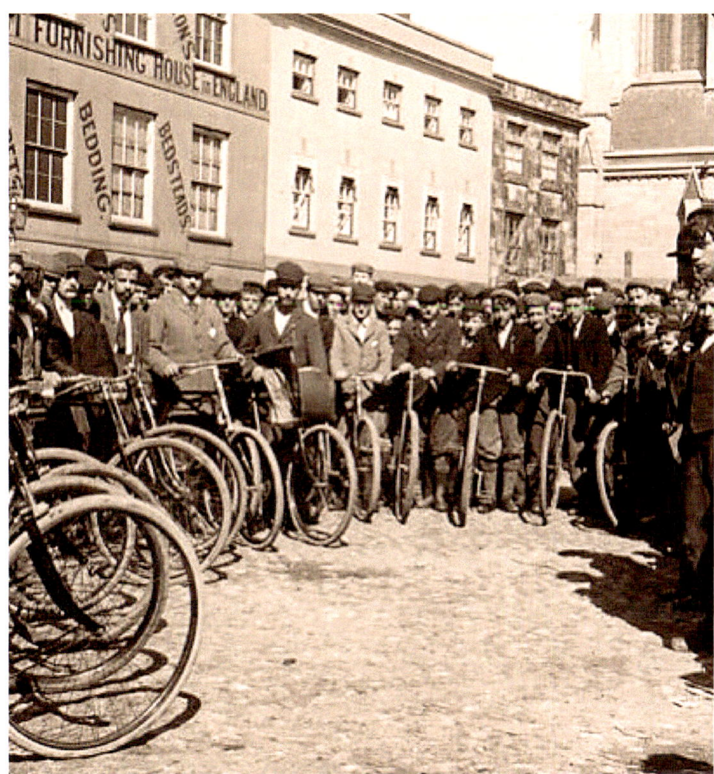

sits today in the nation's capital, a circular rail was constructed for Trevithick's *Catch Me Who Can* in what was known as the 'London Experiment'. All this predated Stephenson's *Rocket* by twenty years.

A Devon man, George Jackson Churchward, was for almost fifty years a leading light in the design of locomotives, and in 1902 became Great Western Railway's locomotive superintendent. In the early 1900s there was much competition between companies wanting to carry the mail from the United States to London. Churchward designed ten engines capable of speedily collecting mail from the ocean liners at Plymouth and transporting it to the capital. In 1903, the *City of Truro* was built to be one of the engines to carry the 'Ocean Mail'. On 9 May 1904, near Wellington in Somerset, while on 'Ocean Mail' duties, *City of Truro* made history by reaching 102.3 miles per hour.

Parrot Talk

In the early 1800s, a hawker who later became a draper caused a stir in Truro. His name was Earl James and he bought his materials in London and Manchester. After his days of hawking, he sold his goods from the Seven Stars Inn and afterwards near the Market Hall. His advertisements about his cheap prices annoyed the other drapers but he thrived.

One day, James's wife was questioned in his absence about his business and a voice under the counter said, 'Ginghams at seven pence a yard.' The inquisitors were told that

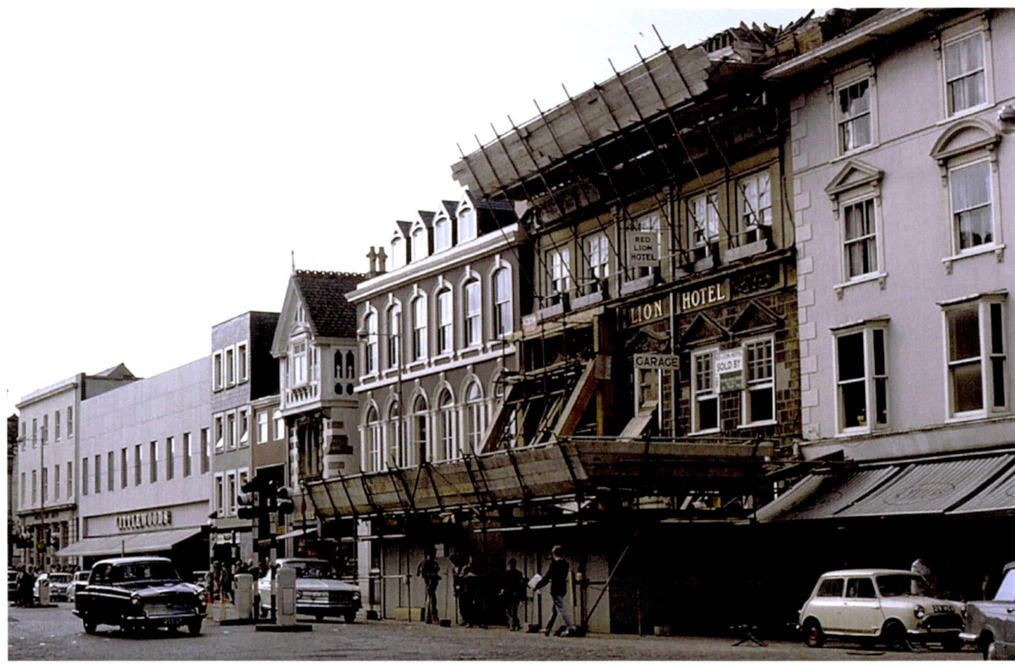

An unusual view of the Red Lion Hotel, which was boarded up after the accident in July 1967.

it was a parrot speaking, and they insisted the bird and all his seven children needed their own licences in order to sell the material. To the amusement of the other customers present, they threatened to inform the authorities of the rule-breaking parrot.

Other members of the James family were also in the drapery trade. His brother called himself the King of Penzance and his nephew called himself the King of Helston, while Earl James proudly styled himself Emperor of Truro.

Thanks to Bert Biscoe, we know that a parrot resided in the Red Lion Hotel for about forty years. On the disastrous day in 1967 when a lorry ran into the front of the hotel while a wedding was being celebrated, there was much relief that no one was hurt save for some injuries for the lorry driver. There were fears for the parrot's safety, but it transpired that he had spent the day outside, his cage having been put out in the fresh air of the back yard.

Spirit of Truro

In 1978, when Truro School pupils were tasked with showing what could be achieved with youthful enthusiasm, they decided to attempt the most challenging feat they could imagine: building a plane.

With the skilful, specialised guidance of Mr Dennis Keam, head of the school's design and technology department, eighty pupils from the fourth and fifth forms took up the project, which was sponsored by the British Petroleum Oils Challenge to Youth Scheme.

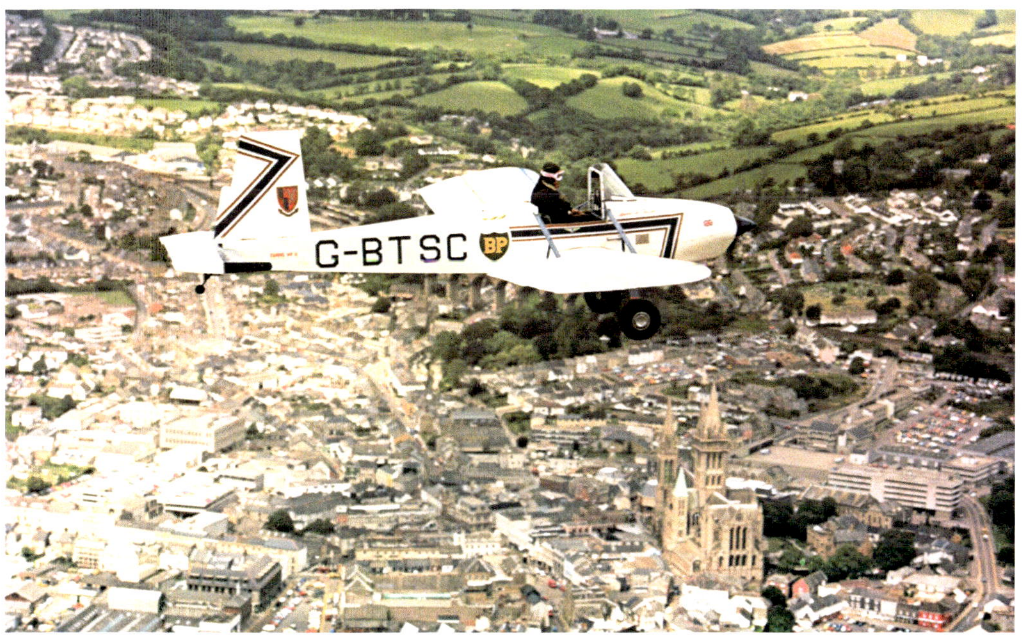

Spirit of Truro seen over the city in June 1981. Constructed by pupils at Truro School under the instruction of teacher Dennis Keam, it was the first aircraft to be built by schoolchildren in Britain.

At a cost of £4,000, it took the schoolboys three years to complete their work, with plans ordered from the United States costing £42. The resulting aircraft, the Evans VP2 two-seater monoplane, is made of wood and powered by an 1834cc modified Volkswagen engine with a top speed of 100 mph. It was named *Spirit of Truro* by Prince Charles in May 1980 when he visited the school to unveil a window in the chapel as part of the school's centenary celebrations.

On 17 June 1981, *Spirit of Truro* made its maiden flight of 25 miles over Truro, circling the school. However, it soon had another flight that wasn't so smooth. Pilot Philip Irish had to make an emergency landing in a field at Goss Moor while

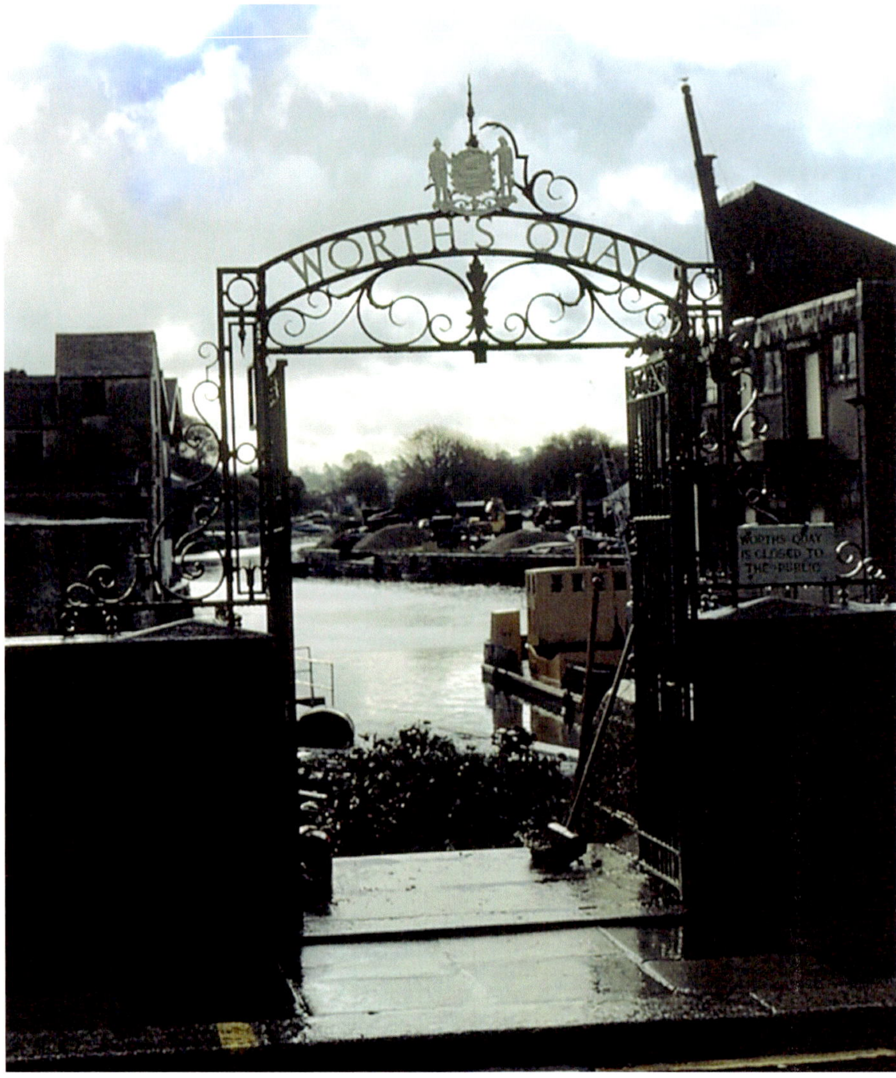

A glimpse of the dredger *Tolverne* through the attractive wrought-iron gateway to Worth's Quay. Unfortunately, this iconic entrance has disappeared since the advent of the bypass.

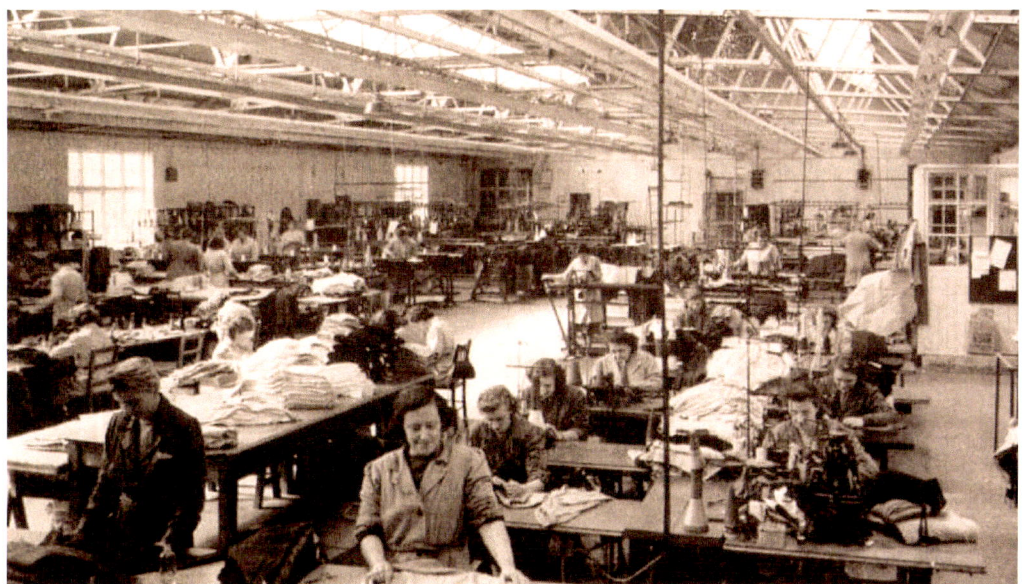

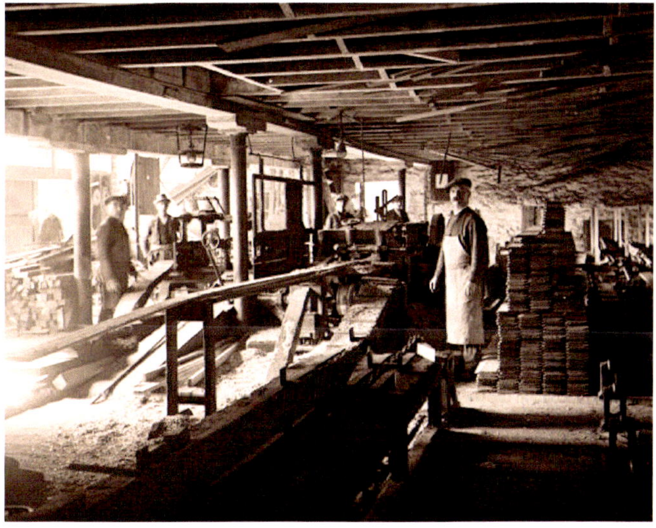

Above: The Knitting Mills at Highertown employed many people and also welcomed customers who called in with their orders. Their closure was a great loss to Truro.

Right: Another important part of Truro's industry that has now gone is Harvey and Company Ltd. They were timber importers and often seasoned timber by floating it in the river. Seen here is one of their workshops in 1923.

flying *Spirit of Truro* to an air display at RNAS Yeovilton in 1981. A fibreglass propeller spinner had come off, causing an engine vibration. It was repaired later in the day, but the aircraft did not make the air display.

A successful flight was accomplished in June 1982 when *Spirit of Truro* crossed the Channel to Morlaix, Truro's twin town in France. The return flight was held back for two days because of bad weather, but *Spirit of Truro* eventually made a safe return. It was a very proud achievement for staff and pupils of Truro School, and the Royal Aeronautical Society later confirmed it was the first flight between the two locations.

Land Rover Update

After the publication of a previous book by the authors, *Secret Truro*, many readers voiced their desire to learn more about the old Land Rover that had ended up buried in a country hedge on a quiet lane between Coosebean and Newmills.

The story was that the owner, Frank Bullen, parked the (now partly visible) vehicle there sometime in the 1980s when it had broken down. Mr Bullen had bought the second-hand Land Rover for £50 and was informed that it was very well travelled; it is believed to have clocked up over 1 million miles, including a journey to Cape Town and back. Bullen had always been too busy repairing Land Rovers for other people, so he didn't get time to repair this one, which had the number plate PAF 808.

When the photo of the Land Rover was shown in *Secret Truro*, John Bennetts recognised the number plate right away and was delighted to shed a little more light on the story.

As a young boy, he accompanied his stepfather to Henry Lawry's garage at Helston where the man purchased the Land Rover brand new in 1951 or 1952. He recalls that the garage was situated on a hill with a showroom that seemed to be underground. Mr Bennetts remembers the occasion vividly because he was frightened by the very noisy macaw that was kept in a large cage there.

At that time, the Bennetts family lived in two caravans and had a horsebox that had been converted into a kitchen. Apparently, the family needed to move

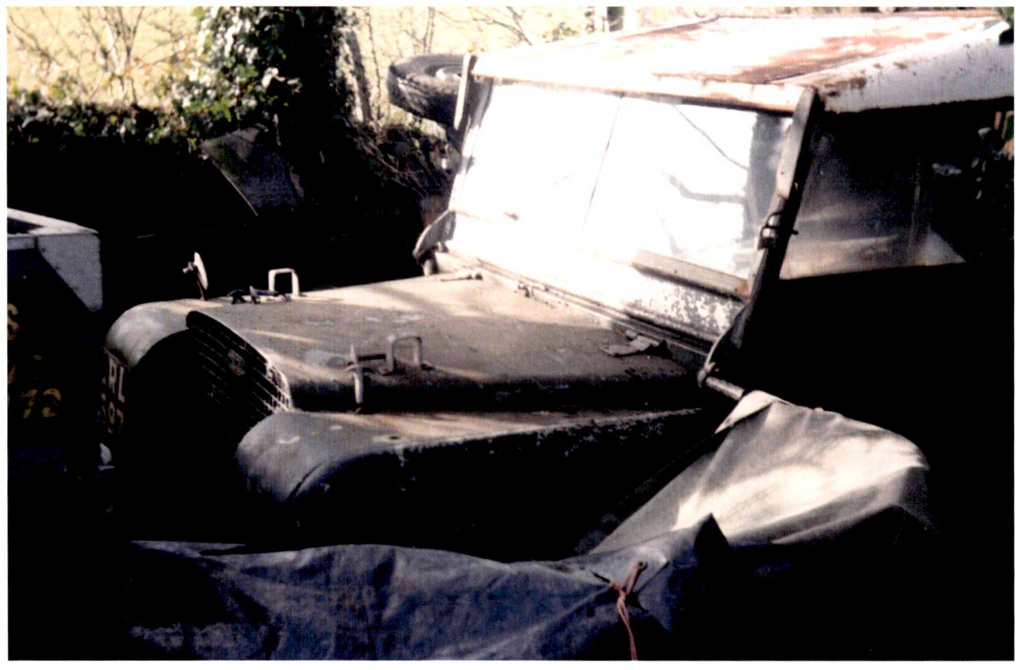

Land Rover enthusiasts will enjoy the photo of this vehicle that is buried deeper into the hedge at Newmills.

residence quite frequently and the purchase of the Land Rover was intended to assist with the moves. Fortunately they never moved very far, usually within a 10-mile radius, and the Land Rover always performed well. Mr Bennetts added to his story that while travelling around in the local area he had spotted a Land Rover with the very similar number plate of PAF 809.

An update on this amusing story has an even quirkier tale to tell. Buried deeper into the hedge is *another* Land Rover with the number plate LRL 597. An interested young cyclist captured a photo of this Land Rover when he spotted it in the hedge several years earlier. Hidden behind this vehicle is a trailer; none have seen daylight for many decades.

So, this unusual sight that has acquired global acknowledgement through the internet, and has been photographed by many, has evoked fond memories for John Bennetts and hopefully will give quirky smiles to many more.

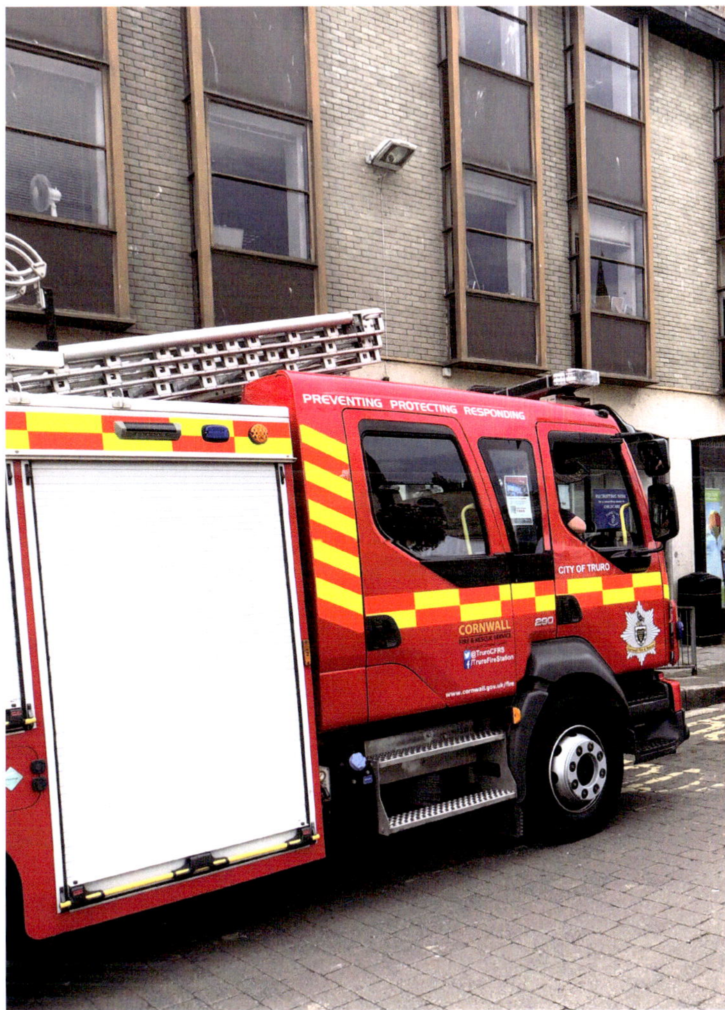

Snapped recently on an event day at the piazza is a City of Truro fire engine, which is a far cry from the first motorised appliance brought to Truro in 1927. Since then, all Truro fire engines have proudly displayed the same title.

Past and Present

Anna Trapnell

Over the years, many famous or well-known people connected to Truro have been written about. However, Anna Keay, author of *The Restless Republic*, a wonderful book about life in England under Oliver Cromwell, tells the story of a woman who is perhaps not so well known.

Anna Trapnell was an outstanding young woman who came to Truro in 1654 to share with the people of Cornwall her devoted Puritan beliefs and powerful religious trances. The Trapnell family were strict Puritans who resided in the London area in a time when many religious groups sprang up throughout the country.

Throughout her childhood Anna had experienced mental illness, often requiring her family to keep a constant watch over her for fear that she might die. As a young woman she would fall into trances and prophesise political upheavals, including the rise and fall of Oliver Cromwell. Her predictions and visions became widespread and soon reached the notice of government. Anna was encouraged to travel to distant Cornwall, where lodgings were arranged for her at Francis Langdon's home, a rural manor a few miles from Truro.

Leonard Welstead, the parish minister of St Ives, was determined to get Anna locked up. He accused her of being a dangerous imposter who incited disorder among the people of Cornwall. When Anna fell into a trance at Truro that had been organised by Welstead, he was quick to get her arrested.

The following day she was to appear before the Truro Sessions of Peace. A crowd had assembled to follow her, some in solidarity and others taunting her. Anna was accused of three crimes: being a vagrant, speaking against the government and holding meetings of evil intent. She pled not guilty to all three. But worse was to come for Anna, with rumours that she was a witch and that she would be tried again for that more serious offence at the quarter sessions. Until that time she was ordered to stay in Cornwall.

When the time came, at the quarter sessions it was decided that Anna should be sent to the city of her birth, but sadly for her this return journey would not take her to the comfort of her own home; she was bound for Bridewell Prison. For the next eight weeks she was to endure the filthy stench, the swarming rats and the company of harlots and thieves. In the end she was released from Bridewell with no charge. Anna had come to Cornwall to promote her faith but her trial at Truro left her with very sad memories of 'Cornhell in the West'.

Betsey Tregaskis

St Clement is a picturesque village on the outskirts of Truro. A few thatched cottages huddle around the church square, while the other part of this quaint and quiet village overlooks the tranquil Tresillian River.

Just inside the entrance to the church lychgate is the slate headstone of Betsey Tregaskis. Although barely legible, the headstone reads, 'In loving memory of Betsey, daughter of William and Elizabeth Tregaskis who died 20 June 1795 aged 19.' It stands against the lychgate wall, as do two or three other headstones, rather than in the consecrated ground of the peaceful churchyard. Mysteriously beautiful flowers are placed around the headstone on the anniversary of Betsey's

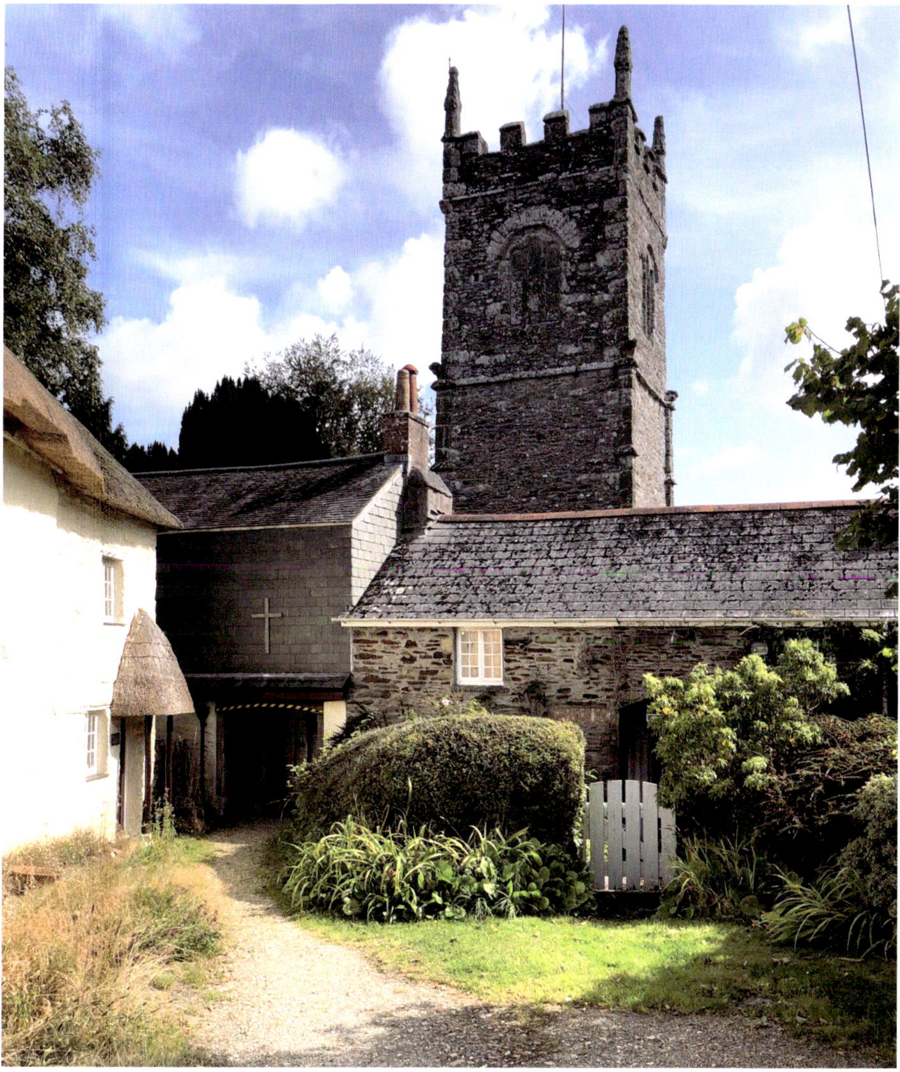

A timeless view of St Clement Church.

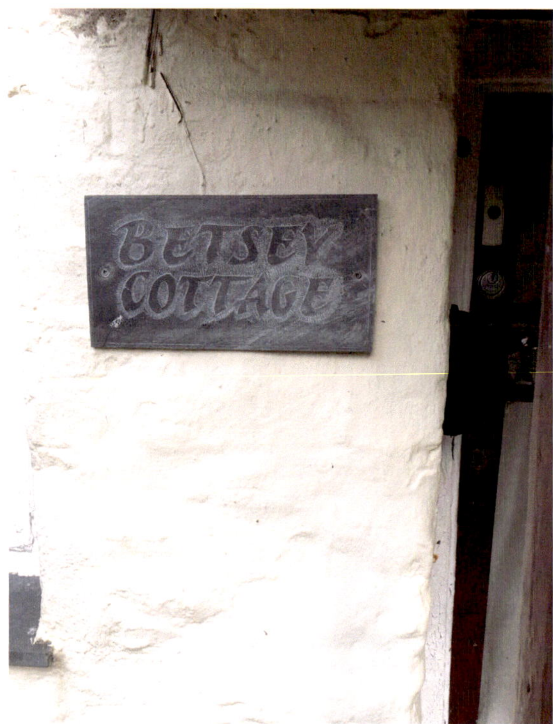

Betsey Cottage, once home to Betsey Tregaskis.

death, but no one seems to know who puts them there. The village residents say the flowers have appeared each anniversary for many years.

This unusual story has inspired local historians to research Betsey's life. Her parents, William and Elizabeth, were known to have run the old inn that was situated close to the entrance of the lychgate. In later years it was known as the Ship Inn. The building is now named Betsey Cottage.

It is believed that young Betsey became pregnant by someone from a different class. During that era this would have brought shame upon her respectable family and rumour has it that, unable to bear the disgrace, she took her own life. Descendants of her family dispute this story, saying that Betsey in fact died from tuberculosis and that is why she was not buried in the churchyard.

The mystery does not end there, for there have been many reports of ghostly sightings and eerie sensations within that area.

One story recalls how members of a coach party visiting the thatched cottages and beautiful church were alarmed to see a young girl standing at the lychgate dressed in a mobcap and old-fashioned dress. At first they thought it was some sort of historical reenactment, but they were assured that there was nothing of that nature going on in the area. This spooky story chimes with the experience of some residents who lived in the nearby Harmony Cottage in the 1960s and experienced paranormal activity in the property.

Whatever the truth, let us hope that poor Betsey now rests in peace.

300-year-old Coins

While digging through the archives of the *West Briton*, the authors were fascinated by an account of a rare acquisition of old coins that appeared in the New Year's Day 1960 edition.

Apparently, H. J. Curnow and T. R. Webb, at that time the proprietors of the antique shop in Pydar Street, had recently acquired from a local businessman a collection of old coins, some of which were of Greek and Roman origin, dating well before Christ. Among the collection, and believed to be of greater interest to Truronians, were some 5-shilling coins that had been minted in Truro during the reign of King Charles I. There were also Cornish pennies that had been minted at various tin mines, but to date Curnow had not had them valued. The collection of coins was examined by H. L. Douch, who was the curator of the museum at that time, and he related that even the museum did not have any of these rare specimens.

Cornish Wrestling

Cornish wrestling has long been a traditional sport of the Cornish, with competitions held all over. Apart from a monetary reward for the victor of such competitions, the greatest prize was fame in the local area.

Many famous or well-known Cornishmen have enjoyed the sport of Cornish wrestling, including theologian John Wesley, inventor Sir Humphry Davy and preacher Billy Bray. One of the best-known wrestlers of the seventeenth century was Richard Stevens, headmaster of the Truro Grammar School, while the aforementioned inventor Richard Trevithick was also a champion wrestler.

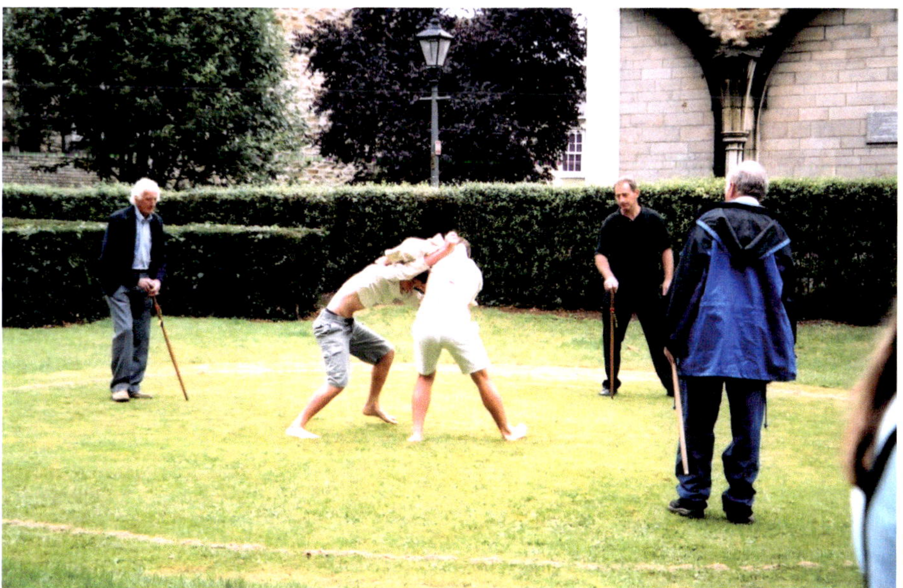

Cornish wrestling in the grounds of Truro Cathedral.

Inns and public houses made good locations for wrestling matches, especially if there was access to a large plat or playing place nearby. The Ship Inn had a wrestling field at the back variously called Caribee Island or the Fair Field. Today it is Moorfield, home to a multi-storey carpark.

In 1825, when three prizes of £5, £3 and a gold-laced hat were offered, the match continued throughout the day, when it was recorded that John Barleycorn and Co. made an appearance and played out some laughable pranks.

During another match in 1829 local ministers protested against the wrestling and made a great disturbance before thousands of spectators. The prize money on that occasion had been £20, £10, £5, £2 and a gold-laced hat, a silver-laced hat and a plain silk hat. Gold-laced hats were often given as first prizes and it is said that the wearers of such hats were immune from the attentions of the press gangs.

In July 1850, a big match was organised behind the Ship, attracting some 8,000 people who turned up to see champion of Cornwall Thomas Gundry. Wrestling matches took place in several locations around Truro and in 1884 matches were staged at Redannick in aid of the infirmary.

The umpires in these matches are known as sticklers, with three of them refereeing each match. The name refers to the long stick that they used to point to any foul moves made by the wrestlers. Threemilestone has a corner which is still known as Sticklers Corner, although it has not been a playing place or wrestling area for many decades.

Startling Tales

Life in Truro was sometimes surprising. In 1854, the youngest brother of printer Mr Netherton was experimenting at home in Lemon Street with a candle and gunpowder when he caused an explosion that shook the street. It is lucky that the

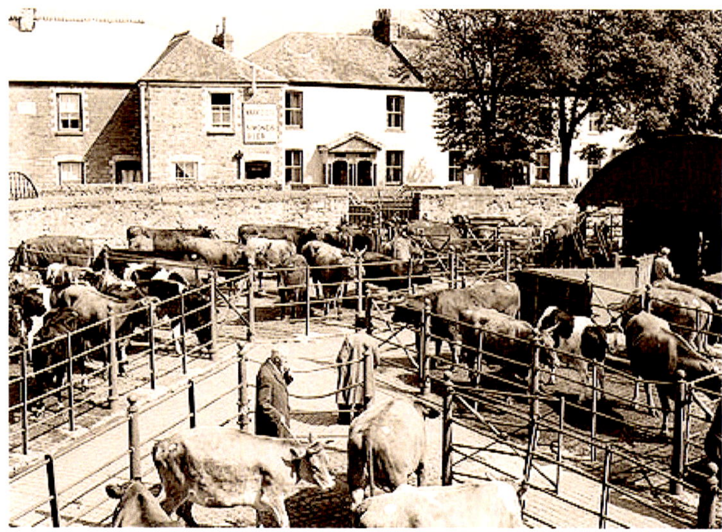

Truro cattle market at the Castle Hill site.

fire engine was not needed, as the gutters that would have supplied it from The Leats happened to be dry at the time.

In 1863, some bullocks near the Lander Monument broke free of the small boy driving them and terrified the vicar of Crowan and his daughter; the following year, a small child was tossed into the air by a spooked bullock.

In these days drovers are no longer seen, but Bob Teague remembers that his grandfather used to drive cattle into town from Coosebean to the cattle market at the top of Castle Hill. Occasionally an animal would be spooked; family memories suggest that one might have run into a house in nearby Edward Street, to the amazement and alarm of the inhabitants.

Pydar Redevelopment

At the time of writing, the upper part of Pydar Street is being redeveloped once more. The first redevelopment took place in the 1960s, and before that this was a well-populated residential area that included Boscawen Row, Moresk Road, the Henry Williams Almshouses, St Mary's School as well as many shops and opes.

Having being buried under tons of concrete and a multi-storey carpark for decades, Boscawen Row was the first site for the archaeologists to excavate during the new redevelopment. This strip of land, dating back to the fifteenth century, was originally owned by the Tregians and stretched from the top of Pydar Street down to the River Allen. At some point it passed to a landowner named Cook and became known as Cook's Lane. In 1820 it was in the ownership of the Boscawens,

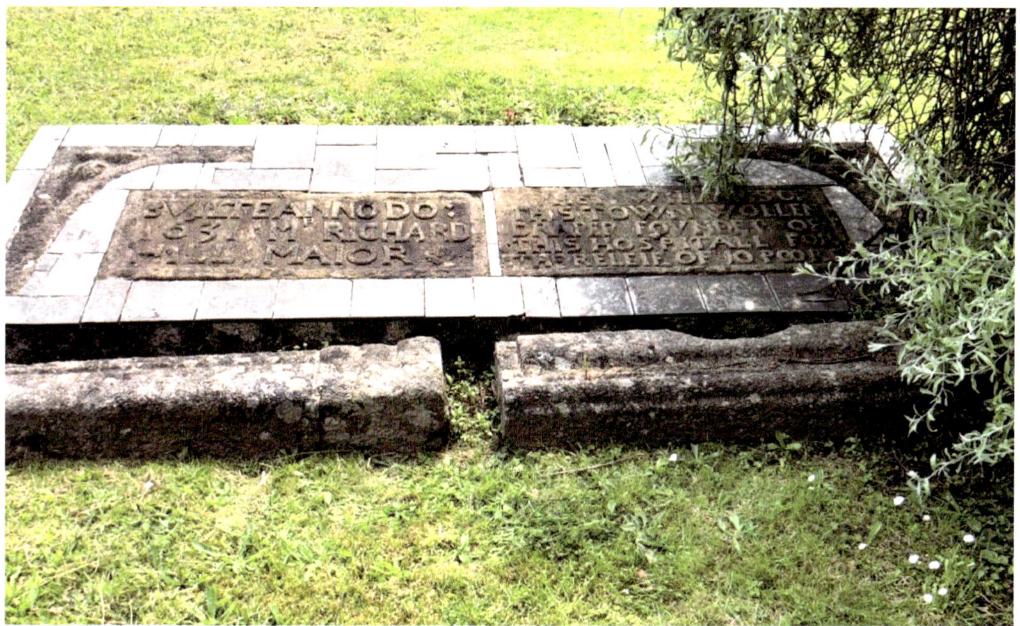

Plaques that once graced the doorway of the old Pydar Street almshouses are now to be found in the garden of Williams Court.

who built a row of cottages that they named after themselves. The census of 1841 noted that most of the occupants were cordwainers or shoemakers.

What was once the widows' meadow was later home to the Town Prison at the Pydar Street end. At the bottom end of the meadow, which was at the rear of Moresk Road, the St Mary's workhouse was once situated. Moresk Road was originally named Street Kedy or Kery, which was the Celtic word for 'walled' or 'fortified', and it was believed to be a causeway road to the castle. The name changed to Goody Street or Goody Lane and then to Goodwives Lane. During this time Mr Arthur Calloway was the Governor of the St Mary's workhouse, and with his wife Betsy was in charge of fifty-nine inmates. In 1851, when the governor of the town prison was Richard Bartlett, records show that only one prisoner was listed. Could crime have been so low at this time?

When the archaeologists had completed their excavations on the Boscawen Row site, they dug the spot where four cottages had once stood at the lower end of the row. The four were once numbered sixteen to nineteen and revealed many interesting finds including a 1950s fireplace that was still in situ at No. 19. A resident who had lived at No. 20 related a story from his father, who was a stoker on the railway. The trains steamed up and down the line on the viaduct

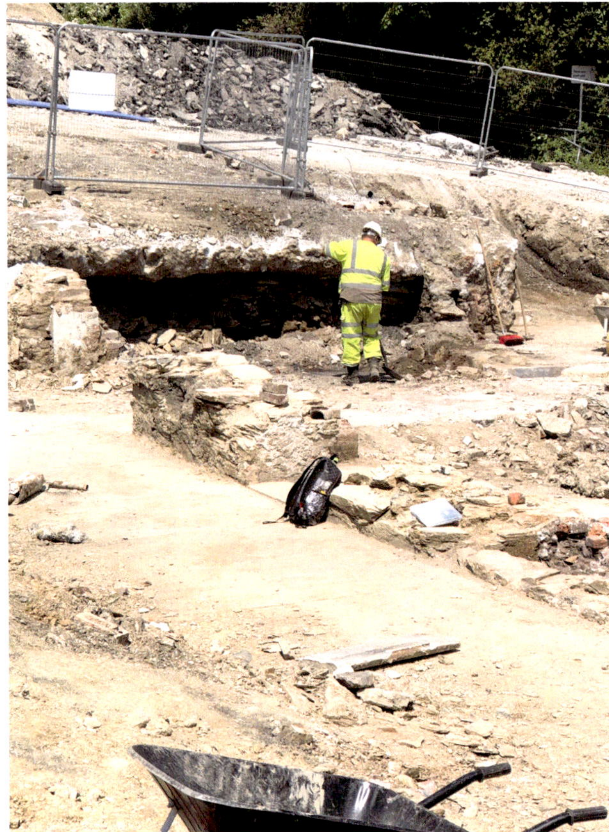

Excavation at the site of the old St Mary's workhouse.

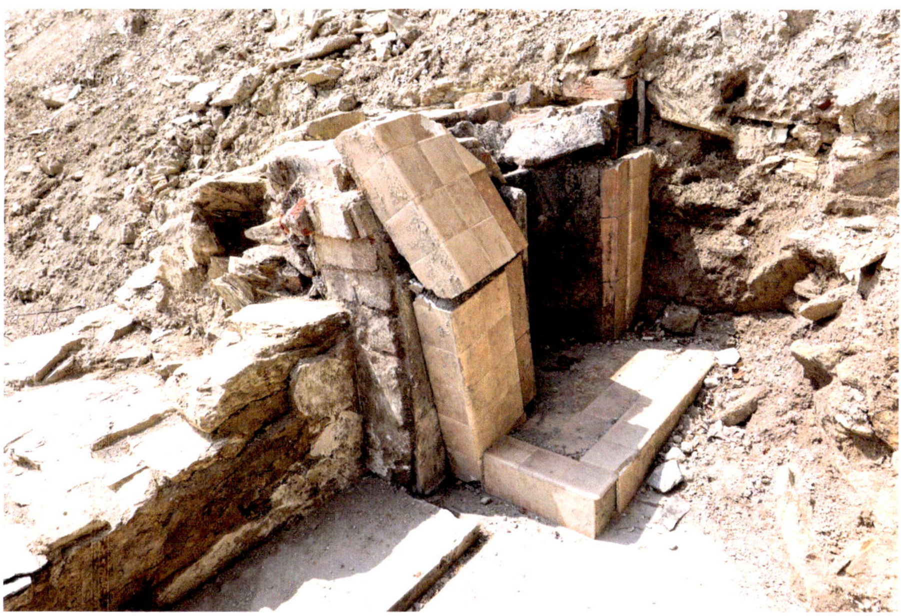

A 1950s fireplace, excavated at the Boscawen Row redevelopment area.

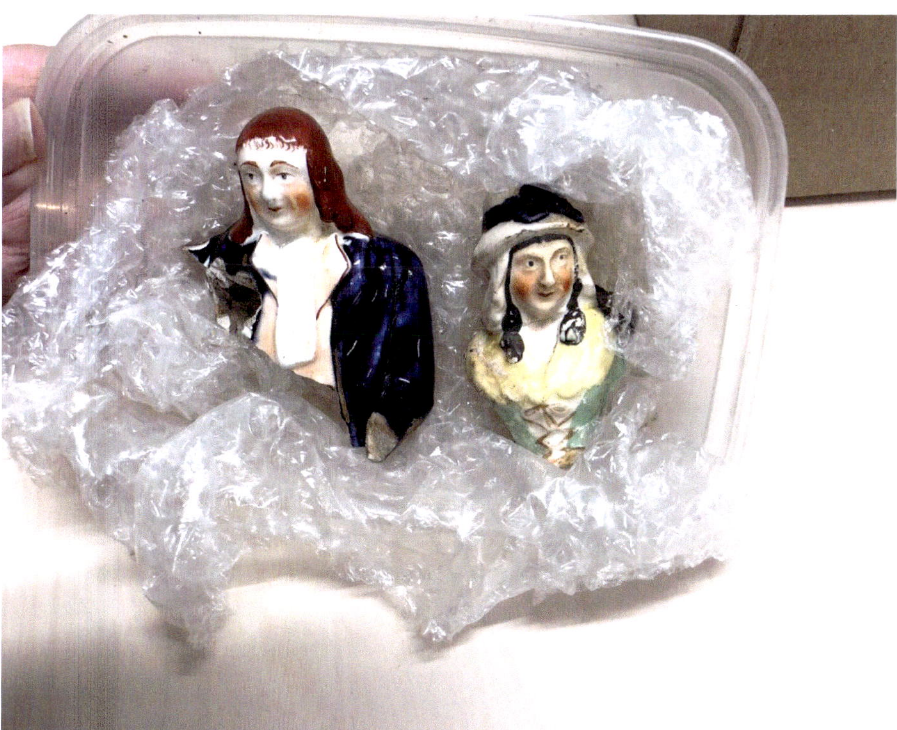

Dickensian ceramic figures found at the old St Mary's Poorhouse 'dig' believed to depict the master and mistress.

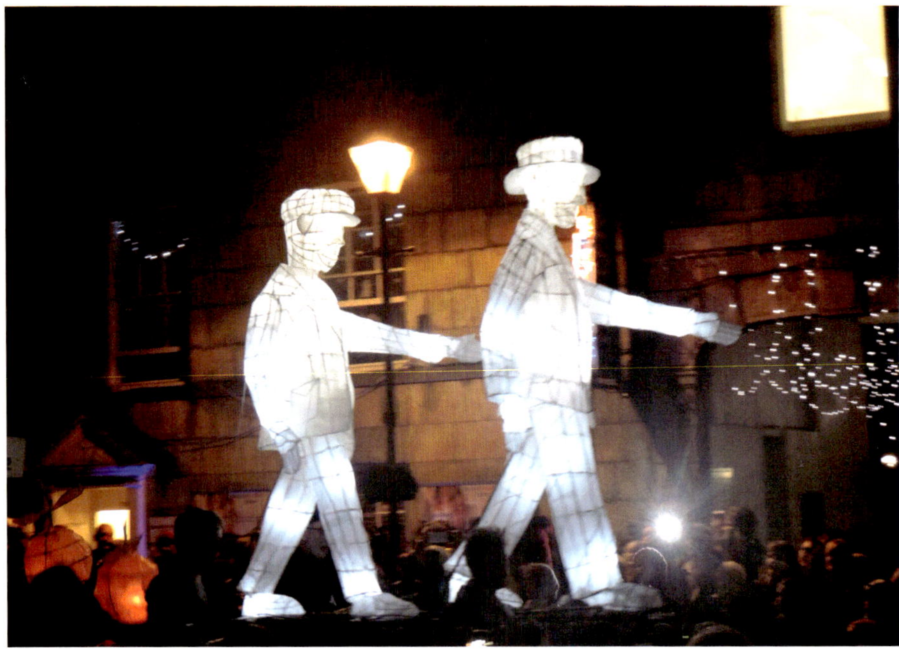

'City of Light' figures that were paraded through the town. Unfortunately, this event no longer takes place.

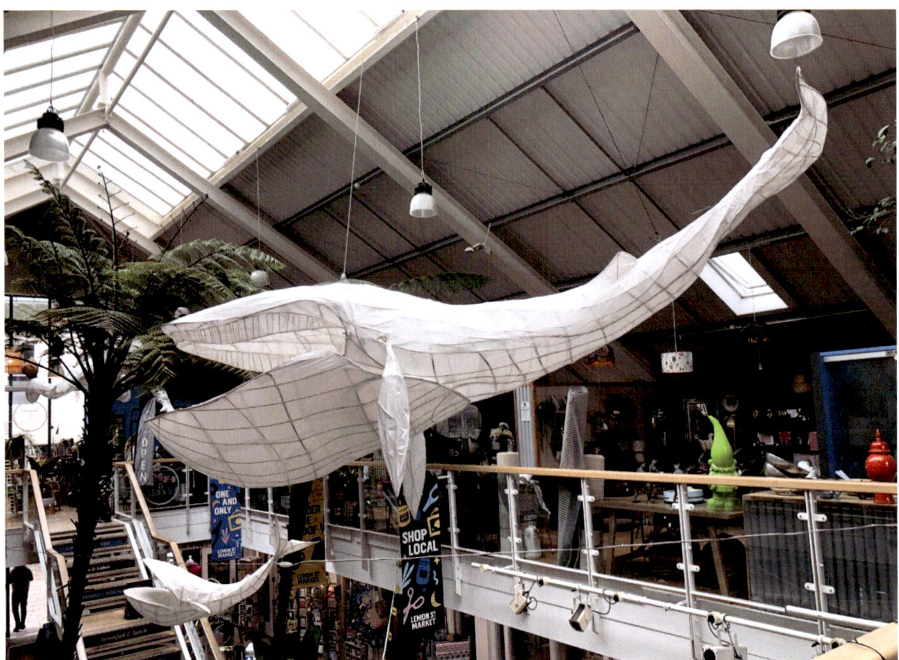

Displayed in Lemon Street Market, this old 'City of Light' exhibit is too admired to be removed.

that was at the back of the row; as the train slowed when they crossed the viaduct on the approach to Truro station, it enabled him to throw large slabs of coal from the engine over the viaduct to the embankment below. His father then collected the coal on his way home for his own fire.

The workhouse site was excavated next, with finds of coins, buttons, marbles, clay pipes and broken bits of medieval pottery. Some coloured ceramic heads of Dickensian characters were also listed in the workhouse artifacts, with the suggestion that they could have been images of the 'Master and Mistress' of the workhouse. The Pop-Up Shop in St Clement Street was the venue for displaying the excavations and in June 2023 pupils from Bosvigo and Archbishop Benson schools were invited to join in the 'dig' and wash and examine the finds. The children were also able to listen to the childhood recollections of a lady who had lived in Boscawen Row throughout the 1950s. Afterwards they made drawings of her stories that will eventually be put in a time capsule which will be buried under the new buildings.

Truro's Town Crier

Truro's town crier, Lionel Knight, is a very well-known and respected character in the town. He and his good wife Carol, who is officially his 'consort', can be frequently seen on special occasions as Lionel performs his duties. Dressed in his smart Cornish black and white outfit, emblazoned with the city's emblem, and accompanied by Carol in her own complementary outfit, he can also be found

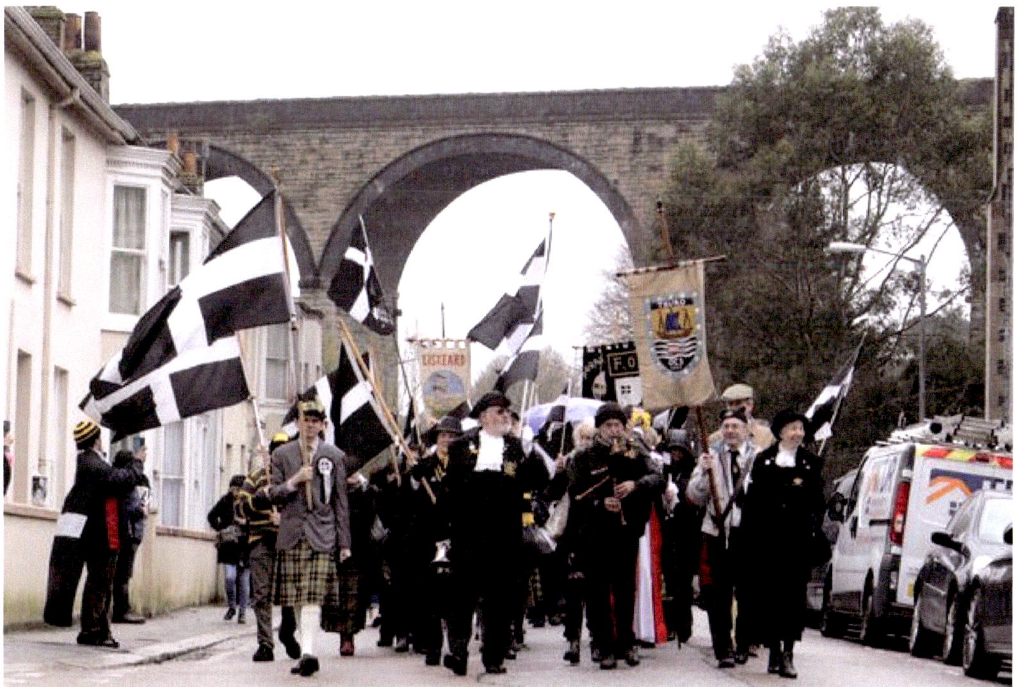

St Piran's Day march in Truro, an annual event on 5 March.

on Wednesdays and Thursdays at the Lemon Coach Park meeting and greeting visitors to the city.

Lionel is a 'proper Trurra boy' who spent his childhood years living in a house belonging to the gasworks that was situated at Gas Hill. His grandfather was a foreman at the gasworks and his father also worked there as a stoker. Lionel has many memories of the area, especially concerning the enormous fire that was caused when a gasometer tank exploded.

Educated at Fairmantle Street School and later at Truro Boys Secondary School, his devotion and loyalty to his home town has been outstanding. In recent years, when Truro's Christmas lights needed renewing and the cost could not be raised by local funds, Lionel stepped up with a generous contribution from his own purse. That Christmas, Truro's streets shone brighter than ever.

A little later, Truro's historic town clock, an iconic landmark that sits proudly atop City Hall, was once again in trouble. The clock tower had started to lean and

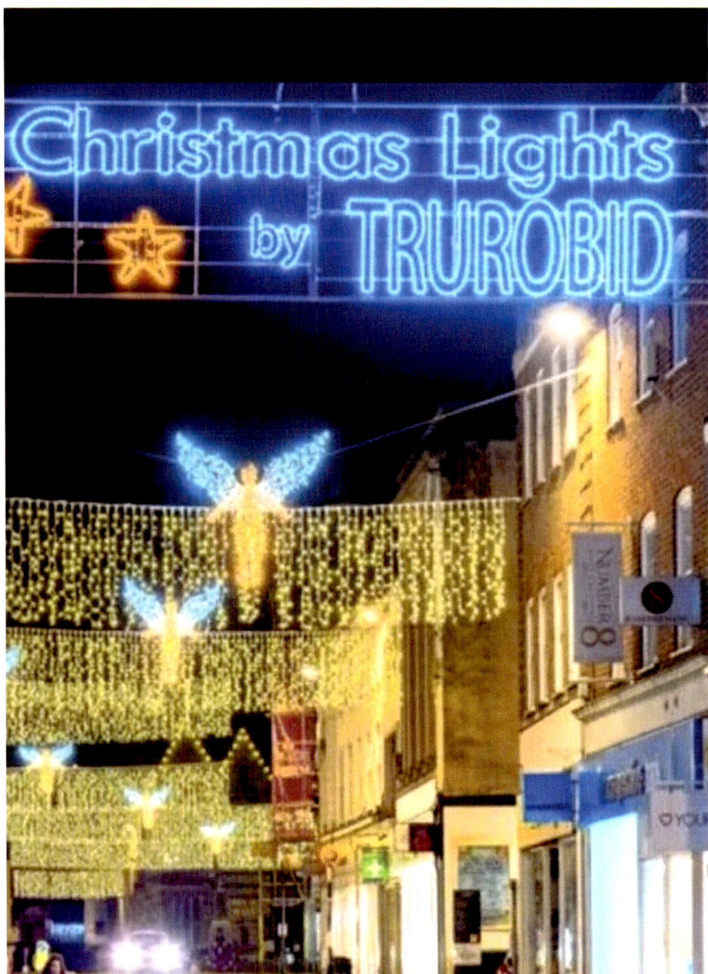

Truro's Christmas decorations welcome the city's shoppers.

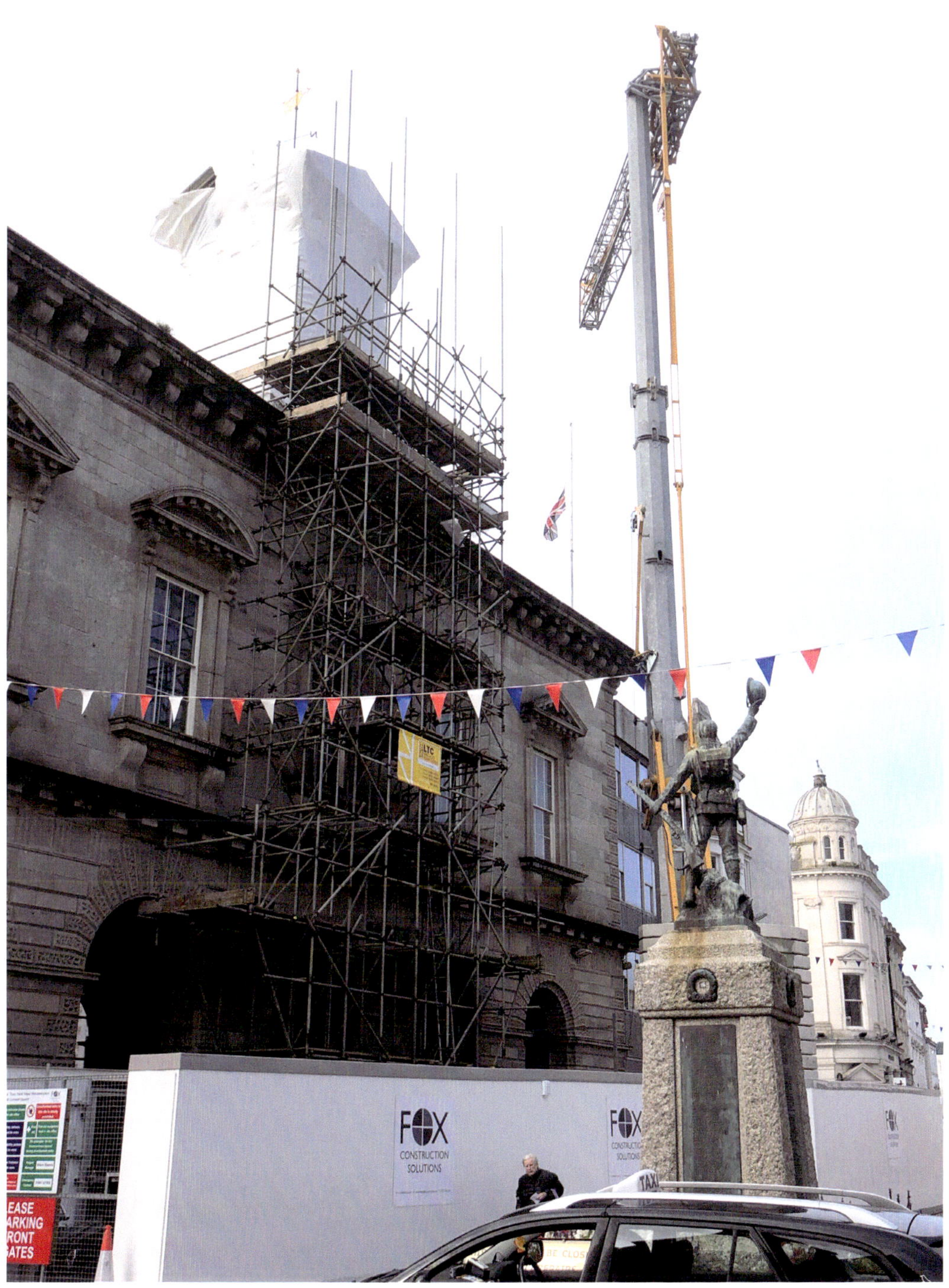

Truro town clock during its recent renovation.

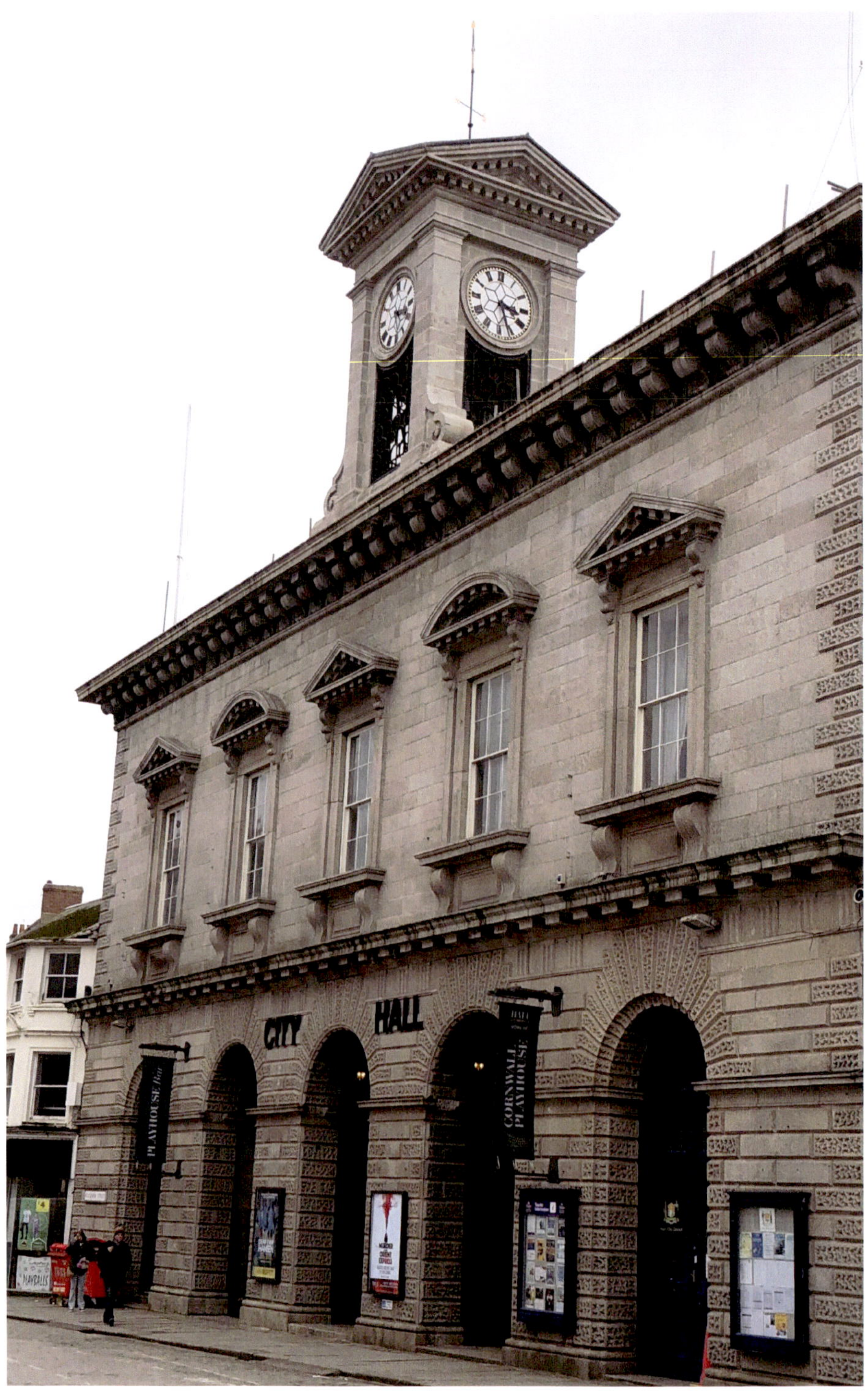

The four-faced clock after renovation.

was in need of urgent repair. The original black-faced clock that was built in 1858 was destroyed by fire in 1914, causing extensive damage to the council chamber below. On that occasion, fortunately, a new white-faced clock was funded by an anonymous donor. This time, however, the whole clock tower was examined by a structural engineer and it was agreed that it needed to be completely rebuilt and the bells refurbished.

Work began in August 2022, and for two years scaffolding surrounded Boscawen Street and the chimes of the town clock were silenced. It was suggested that the town didn't need a clock anymore, but Lionel stood his ground and insisted that it was a very important part of the city. Once again he donated a considerable sum of money, and now, splendidly repaired, it once again graces the rooftops and smiles down with its four faces. With loud chimes it sings out grateful thanks to our town crier: 'Oyez, oyez, thank you Lionel!'

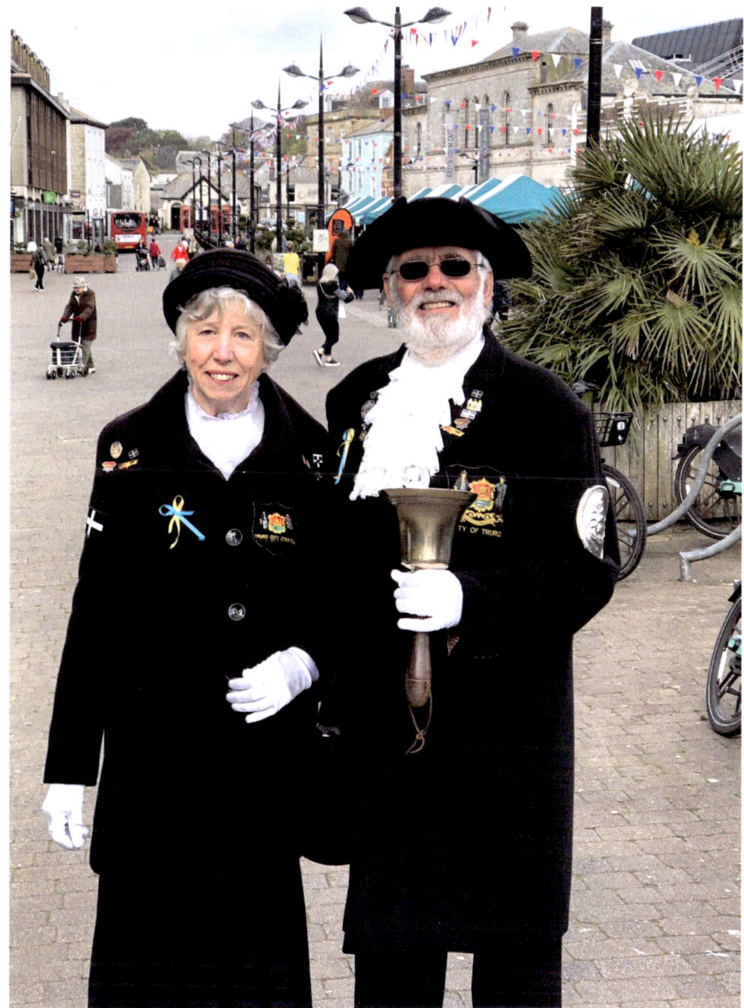

Truro's town crier Lionel Knight, and his consort Carol.

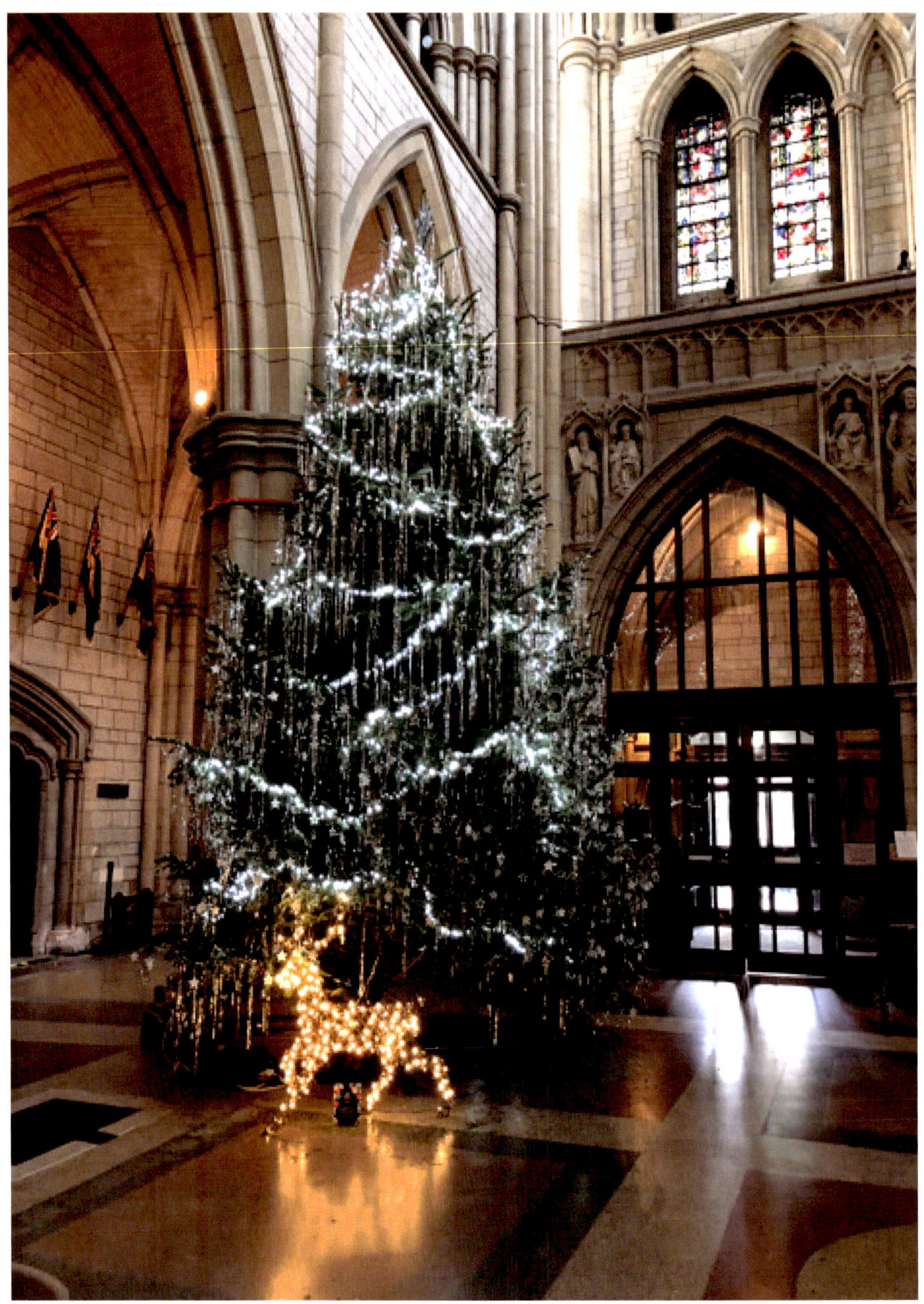

The traditional Christmas tree inside Truro Cathedral 2024 is once again a joy to see.